BOLLINGEN SERIES XLV

The Collected Works of Paul Valéry

Edited by Jackson Mathews

VOLUME II

PAUL VALÉRY

OCCASIONS

Translated by
Roger Shattuck and Frederick Brown

With an Introduction by
Roger Shattuck

BOLLINGEN SERIES XLV · II

PRINCETON UNIVERSITY PRESS

THIS IS VOLUME ELEVEN OF THE
COLLECTED WORKS OF PAUL VALÉRY
CONSTITUTING NUMBER XLV IN BOLLINGEN SERIES
SPONSORED BY BOLLINGEN FOUNDATION.
IT IS THE ELEVENTH VOLUME OF
THE COLLECTED WORKS TO APPEAR

Library of Congress catalogue card no. 56-9337
ISBN 0-691-09856-5
Type composed at the University Printing House, Cambridge, England
Printed in the United States of America
by Princeton University Press, Princeton, N.J.
DESIGNED BY ANDOR BRAUN

CONTENTS

IL DÉPEND DE CELUI QUI PASSE
QUE JE SOIS TOMBE OU TRÉSOR
QUE JE PARLE OU ME TAISE
CECI NE TIENT QU'À TOI
AMI N'ENTRE PAS SANS DÉSIR

TOUT HOMME CRÉE SANS LE SAVOIR
COMME IL RESPIRE
MAIS L'ARTISTE SE SENT CRÉER
SON ACTE ENGAGE TOUT SON ÊTRE
SA PEINE BIEN-AIMÉE LE FORTIFIE

DANS CES MURS VOUÉS AUX MERVEILLES
J'ACCUEILLE ET GARDE LES OUVRAGES
DE LA MAIN PRODIGIEUSE DE L'ARTISTE
ÉGALE ET RIVALE DE SA PENSÉE
L'UNE N'EST RIEN SANS L'AUTRE

CHOSES RARES OU CHOSES BELLES
ICI SAVAMMENT ASSEMBLÉES
INSTRUISENT L'ŒIL À REGARDER
COMME JAMAIS ENCORE VUES
TOUTES CHOSES QUI SONT AU MONDE

ON THE PASSERBY DEPENDS
WHETHER I AM TOMB OR TREASURE HOUSE
WHETHER I SPEAK OR REMAIN MUTE
IT RESTS WITH YOU ALONE
FRIEND DO NOT ENTER WITHOUT DESIRE

EVERY MAN CREATES UNWITTINGLY
AS HE BREATHES
BUT THE ARTIST FEELS HIMSELF CREATE
THE ACT ENGAGES ALL HE IS
HIS CHOSEN SUFFERING STRENGTHENS HIM

WITHIN THESE WALLS DEVOTED TO WONDERS
I WELCOME AND PROTECT THE WORK
OF THE ARTIST'S MIRACULOUS HAND
EQUAL AND RIVAL OF HIS MIND
THE ONE IS NOTHING WITHOUT THE OTHER

RARE THINGS OR BEAUTIFUL THINGS
HERE KNOWINGLY ASSEMBLED
TEACH THE EYE TO SEE
AS IF IT NEVER YET BEHELD
ALL THINGS THAT ARE IN THE WORLD

Inscriptions for the Palais de Chaillot

Paul Valéry: Sportsman and Barbarian

WHEN A MAN becomes a public institution, he has either abdicated his personality and privacy or arranged his "back shop" so securely that no one can disturb him. In the case of Paul Valéry it all happened swiftly just as he was entering his fifties. He appears to have thrived on prominence.

The death in February, 1922, of Édouard Lebey, the cultivated businessman for whom he had worked as "private secretary" for twenty years, coincided with the events that established Valéry's literary fame. A few months earlier, over three thousand readers of the literary review *Connaissance* had named him the greatest contemporary French poet, on the basis of two slender volumes in limited editions. In May, 1922, *Le Divan* published a special number honoring Valéry with contributions by André Gide, Henri de Régnier, François Mauriac, Charles du Bos, and Anna de Noailles. A major collection of new poems, *Charmes*, appeared the following month. That autumn, responding both to his need for a new source of income and to the call of literary celebrity, he began a series of lecture engagements. For the next twenty years, until his death, he spent a substantial portion of his time aboard trains and on lecture platforms across the entire continent of Europe. By 1924 he had assembled a collection of essays and lectures for publication under the title *Variété*. That was also the year in which Anatole France died. The Dada-Surrealist group, toward whom Valéry had been cordial a few years earlier, welcomed France's death as a release of the present from the burden of the past; their public demonstrations of delight outraged the official guardians of French culture. But Valéry was not among the demonstrators. For it was he who succeeded France in two positions he left vacant: as a member of the French Academy and President of the French P.E.N. Club. Thus Valéry stepped symbolically into the role of poet laureate of the Third Republic. Its life-span was to coincide with his. From that time on, every official honor and duty fell to him automatically. He complained in 1932 of being "a kind of state poet." He had thirteen more years of it.

Fortunately, Valéry was safe. He had prepared his retreat. Between five A.M. when he rose and mid-morning, his time was his own. The matutinal man belonged to no one else. The wonder of it will long remain. No proper biography, official or unofficial, has yet appeared to tell the tale. More than a hundred books have been written about Valéry—about his mind, his poetics, his work, his painting. But no life. It is ironically appropriate that the best source of information on him is the compressed chronology that opens the first volume of the Pléiade edition of his works. Later references will be to this edition. Even in those pages the emphasis falls on his intellectual career, the story of his mind. One has to look far afield to discover anything about his other activities: his sensitive pencil drawings, his lifelong love of swimming, the bicycling he enjoyed as a young man, his love-life (he had one), and the fact that he composed much of his published prose directly on a typewriter. Valéry himself tells us why all these things are relevant. In the "Note and Digression" on Leonardo da Vinci, he taxes literary criticism and criminology with the same fundamental error:

treating a man as the *cause* of what he does. An author, like a criminal, is rather the *effect* of his works.

It is difficult to tell just how seriously this literary institution came to take himself. A good number of people have retailed the story about his reluctance to be satisfied with the customary hand-me-down uniform when he was elected to the French Academy; he had one made to order, of elegant cut. Yet the creature of ceremony was clearly not the whole man. François Valéry relates how his father at the family dinner table liked to refer to himself as a "government anarchist" and had blunt words for the mighty men of state he began to see more and more often: "They don't know any more than anyone else. They're all buffoons." It is hard to gauge the streak of imposture and flippancy that runs through all his writings, particularly *Mon Faust*.

The real question may not lie in the direction of Valéry's "seriousness." Laughter he referred to as "a kind of intellectual vomiting"; yet it is textually evident that he approached most public performances with his tongue well in cheek and a strong sense of self-parody. He would have dismissed all these matters as beside the point; they belong to literary history, the "external politics" of a writer. Nevertheless, even though his back room was secure and steadily occupied, the externals make their own special revelation. His career, in fact, resembles a compounding of Montaigne's, who quit "the dance" of public life at least twice in order to write, with Rimbaud's, who quit literature for keeps in his early twenties and found his way into gunrunning. Valéry's poetic production was confined to two brief periods: the first very early, before he turned twenty-one (1887–92), the other in his forties (1912–22). After each period came twenty years of highly active "silence" in prose. His daily life evidently followed a comparable alternation between solitary work and a full social calendar. In a letter to Gide in 1929, Valéry identified the geological or ecological formation that allowed him to survive when he was inundated by the great ocean of public life: "The bottom layers, the foundation hasn't changed. You know that part is simple and straightforward. But between Me and me, one thing and another has raised a ring of coral. I'm an Atoll."

In my own experience I have found that the process of reading and absorbing Valéry observes an alternating rhythm comparable to that of his life. Usually one begins with the poetry and responds to the sensuous flesh and fiber of his best poems. Later, an inevitable reaction leaves one cool to the narcissistic repetitiousness of his inferior verse and to the mock dignity of certain speeches. Then, after an interval of absence, one returns to find in his work a surprisingly harmonious and unified monument of the mind. Contrary to much that has been said and written, Valéry's long dialogue with mathematics and science does not represent a flirtation or a useless humbug. To ridicule his serious application to these studies, and his friendship with Einstein and Bergson, with Poincaré and Vallery-Radot and Jean Perrin and other contemporary men of science, is to miss the value of his exceptional sensibility. From his youthful investigations of Poe and Leonardo down to his last lecture on Voltaire, Valéry emphasized the simple truth that specialization belongs to our technological civilization and not to the mind itself. In 1925 he wrote to the physicist Charles Henry: "Because you feel the prick of relativity, you have undertaken to discover the reciprocal relations between all phenomena, not only physical but also sensory and psychic, to the very limit of possibility. Nothing could appeal to me more, for the ruling thought of my entire life has been to try to represent such a general relation of symmetry and to discover consequences applicable to culture and even to art."

The proof lies in the notebooks that cover fifty years. In page after page of prose paragraphs that lead to equations, he put into practice what he declared from the start: that he wanted "to amuse myself by translating everything into mathematics." But it was no mere matter of amusement. His early and enduring conviction that such relations as relativity, simultaneity, reciprocity, symmetry, interference, and periodicity belong to the mind as much as to any other part of nature expresses his genius better than his clever pronouncements on politics or the rules of versification. I should judge that, poetically as well as philosophically, Valéry's early reading of William Thomson (Lord Kelvin) on the composition of the ether and of Clerk Maxwell on the sorting demon was as important as his study of Poe and Huysmans and Mallarmé.

But Valéry was never inclined to sacrifice humanism to mere scientism. In the academic set speech on "Prizes for Virtue," he introduces a fictional character who comes from the Companion of Sirius and represents the "point of view" of that distant star. (Valéry is gently mocking Ernest Renan.) But far from exposing the relativity of all virtues and ideals, this imaginary inquirer discovers the true nature and value of Christian charity and carries that startling news back to where he came from. The best of what men have slowly created through history is worth defending against the encroachment of mindless relativism. Close behind Valéry's apparent detachment lie both conviction and courage.

II

A myth, fostered by Valéry in the 1924 preface to the first volume of *Variété*, has it that he wrote his poetry entirely for himself, with no plans for publication, and that all his prose was written by invitation on assigned subjects. This contrast of private poetry and public prose corresponds exactly to the symbolist doctrine stemming from Baudelaire and Mallarmé that there are two languages: vernacular journalism and poetry. As one might expect, the distinction breaks down in practice, and it is just as well. Valéry's most important prose works, *Monsieur Teste* and *Mon Faust*, were neither of them "occasional." On the other hand it was the persistent solicitation and encouragement of Gide, who wanted to publish Valéry's early poetry, that drove him back to writing verse and led to the completely new poem, *La Jeune Parque*. The whole magnificent volume, *Charmes*, grew out of that complex occasion. Later, of course, the official Valéry became a victim of circumstance in every sense and was highly aware of it. In February, 1927, four months before his formal reception into the French Academy, he was at work on the speech "praising" his predecessor, Anatole France. He wrote as follows to Gide:

I'm writing five things at once and everyone thinks the France speech is finished before it's even begun. And then we have to help settle Claude's family, plan Agathe's wedding, go out to dinner, go out to lunch—be toastmaster at the Perrin banquet, participate in the Spinoza ceremonies (!) and type, type forever on the Oliver, type a Stendhal, type a Mallarmé, type a Europe, type a Lafontaine, type a Paris,

type an Alphabet, type, type, type....I realize now that
I pay for everything with ideas—and those imbeciles are
forever asking me for something high-flown or lengthy, the
kind of thing that runs me ragged....

Still, much as they may have harassed him, these command
performances and set pieces for official functions provided
Valéry with more than a needed source of income. Each one
made certain formal demands on him, sometimes with good
results. For example, the strict terms governing the text on
architecture asked of him in 1921 (115,800 characters to fit a
special format) led him to adopt the dialogue form (*Eupalinos
or the Architect*) which he went on to use to good advantage.
An increasing portion of his reading and thinking was under-
taken "on order"—and we need not regret the fact. For I
believe that the occasional nature of Valéry's production
saved him from his two most serious intellectual vices:
silence and monomania. Without the insistence of friends
and the lucrative commissions, Valéry might well have left
us only his notebooks, unclassifiable either as literary works
or as the systematic study of a subject. And even the note-
books would have been the poorer. A constant succession of
new contexts, however, forced him to modify the arrange-
ment and the lighting of his ideas; he was perpetually coming
upon a new approach or a fresh metaphor out of empathy
with his audience. Monsieur Teste, Valéry's fond caricature
of a solitary genius or prince of all intellectual charlatans,
never produced anything except his own exasperating "plas-
ticity" of thought, a counterfeit letter from his wife, a ten-
page Log Book, and hours on end of concentrated sleep. No
one asked any more of him. But much more was asked
of Valéry. Though he did not have to be locked in a room

with sheets of blank paper (as was the case with Anatole France), the deadline was his negative inspiration. It provided his extensive prose work with the equivalent of rhyme in poetry: "a law independent of the subject and comparable to an external timepiece." From verse to verse, from platform to platform, the writer rises to the occasion.

Both the most prominent and the most neglected example of Valéry's piecework is the set of inscriptions he produced for the new Palais du Trocadéro (known today as the Palais de Chaillot) in 1937. Remembering his fruitful experience with *Eupalinos*, he insisted that the commission be given precise terms. The architect asked for four texts of five lines each, not exceeding thirty-seven characters to a line. These seven-hundred-odd letters were to be carved in stone for all Paris to see during the years to come, on a public building housing a museum and theater. Literature by the meter; yet we have no living tradition of lapidary style. Valéry's performance astonishes in its mastery of the genre, unless one looks through collections of his fragmentary texts like *Mélange* and *Tel Quel*. He might have been writing inscriptions for public buildings and private retreats all his life, at the foot of his notebook pages.

Action is a fleeting madness.

The most precious thing a man has is a brief epilepsy.

Genius lasts only an instant.

Love is born of a look; and one look is enough to beget eternal hatred.

This jotting takes on the permanence of granite; the words could have been graven on an opera house—or a mental institution.

The Palais de Chaillot inscriptions come tantalizingly close to poetry; their disposition and style oblige one to read the lines as individual verses. All but one have an even number of syllables. (In fact an earlier version of the second line, published in the *Nouvelles Littéraires*, has ten syllables: *Que je sois une tombe ou un trésor*.) The fourth inscription comes out as a perfectly regular unrhymed five-line stanza. The syntax, which grows into something deliberately complex and crabbed in much of Valéry's work, both prose and poetry, here displays an utter clarity even without benefit of punctuation. And the text stands up under the immense weight of attention focused on it; every word counts, literally.

A building, he says softly, offers itself directly to the individual passerby, with a promise of riches to him who holds the secret of observation: that secret is desire. This building houses the handiwork of men we call artists because they, more than anyone else, are aware of what they do. Their very awareness makes their acts more entire and confers on them a lucidity that is both painful and consoling. The works housed in these walls all flow from a man's hand, most marvelous of organs; the direct extension, instrument, and agent of his thought. Ears, eyes, mouth—these organs behold and confront the world. Only the hand *makes*. And the rare or beautiful things the hand makes teach us to see everything else in the world afresh.

These limpid commonplaces convey the very essence of Valéry. He is attitudinizing and perorating less on the face of this public building than he sometimes does in his informal essays. The little miracle of this text is to have expressed it all—all Valéry's thought on the attentiveness of the individual spectator, on the artist as conscious of his making, on the symbiotic link between hand and thought, on art not as embodying eternal and autonomous aesthetic value but as producing an effect. A work of art calls attention to itself in order to reveal *the world*. These twenty lines declare what it is not always easy to discern in reading his beautifully chiseled verse: that Valéry cannot be classified as the last great devotee of art for art's sake. This most institutional of occasions permitted Valéry to stand completely at ease on the unmapped frontier that connects journalism to poetry, elevated sentiments to intimacies, the creative spirit to the public act, the body to the mind.

If one compares these four inscriptions to Valéry's two principal formal speeches, made in the full pomp of the French Academy, the public man comes off poorly. I partly concur in Edmund Wilson's petulant criticisms of Valéry's reception speech. The formalities have little polish. The coyness with which he avoids mentioning Anatole France by name, and the smirk with which he calls his predecessor a "classical writer," make the speech more evasive than incisive. The two promising ideas it broaches (the book as an "instrument of pleasure" offering a perfect instant; the suggestion that "doubt begets form") never take full shape. Valéry misjudged the occasion and his own talents.

From all accounts the speech welcoming Pétain to the Academy in 1931 was more impressive in performance. The text stands up well as a piece of writing appropriate to the occasion and surpassing it. Hindsight shows us that Pétain's legendary sagacity had already failed him when he was elected to the Academy. For, quite apart from his political role in coming to terms with the Germans between 1939 and 1944, one has to reckon with the catastrophically wrong-headed influence he had in lulling the country to sleep behind the Maginot line and in refusing to recognize the revolutionary implications of mechanized warfare. But in 1931 the great general's glory was still unclouded. Valéry narrates the events of his career effectively and eloquently; the audience must have followed his periods with rapt attention. And he hangs the tale around the supreme commonplace of military science: *le feu tue*—gunfire kills. Pétain's secret was to have discovered the obvious. Though it is annoying to read of how Pétain and Valéry compared notes and read their speeches aloud to each other in advance of the event, Valéry produced a subtle text that has two effects. First, it turns our attention toward the phenomenon of the military mind which had long interested him. It turns out to be Foch's mind with its swift grasp of essentials and its impatience to act that really impressed Valéry. (The irony of this occasion turned on the fact that Pétain had been elected to succeed his archenemy, Foch, and had to eulogize him for two hours. Pétain did not attempt any of the subtleties Valéry had used in praising Anatole France.) The second effect of the speech about two generals must have been very carefully calculated. Valéry's passionate patriotism in describing his country's behavior in the first World War turns out to be the intellectual stronghold from which to denounce the horror, the fascination, and the unthinkability of war. His rhetorical address in the second person to Pétain sitting next to him "under the Cupola" earns him the right to speak out against man's greatest self-deception. Pétain was a cold, authoritarian figure with an orderly but lackluster mind; Valéry's portrait inflates him to exaggerated greatness.

But on the larger international issues, Valéry's political instinct was sound and eloquent, at a time when once again Europe was beginning to drift toward war.

The most successful texts contained in the present volume of occasional writing are the "Address to the Congress of Surgeons," "A Personal View of Science," and the short reply to the Surrealists' questionnaire on suicide. In addressing the surgeons, Valéry made a few preliminary flourishes and then advanced unhesitatingly toward the underground aspects of surgery: the liturgical atmosphere of an operation, fainting at the sight of blood or of an incision in the body, the interference between knowledge and the functioning of natural processes, and, as in the Palais de Chaillot inscriptions, the magic that resides in the human hand. "A Personal View of Science" consists for the most part of a lucid exposition of what has happened to technique and theory in modern science, plus some comparisons that are entirely Valéry's. Confronted by the assigned subject of suicide, he turns into a scenario writer. What comes out is the outline for a short story by Poe: suicide by self-fascination. In these three cases, the occasion served everyone's purpose including Valéry's. The texts convey a sense of ease and enjoyment in the writing.

III

Few critics have tried to tell us anything about Valéry as a writer of French prose even though his essays appear to be as widely read as his poetry. There is a dense forest of interpretation around his writings in verse, and several intelligent critics have examined his aesthetics and his poetics. But apart from a few remarks about his occasional Italian turn of phrase and the "opacity" of his prose, one gets the impression that his style must be nondescript. It is a serious error. What characterizes his prose most is the variety, in kind and quality, of the styles Valéry can muster. All the formal speeches are larded with asides, brief skirmishes with the audience that play for a laugh. In these passages, Valéry's "I" hovers between the mocking Academician, the serious "man in the mind," and the straightforward human being. Only in the Pétain speech is his rhetoric sustained and effective; he was being didactic. In contrast, the short text on suicide and the somewhat more developed article on "The Future of Literature" waste no time on preliminaries or lengthy transitions. Valéry divides suicides into three classes and examines them one after another as if before a class. Then, instead of imagining himself in the situation of delivering a speech and padding it out with dramatic asides, he imagines himself convincingly in the very act of committing suicide. As a result his two columns are more arresting than the surrounding texts by surrealist activists in the pages of *La Révolution surréaliste*. When he bends his attention to the social evolution of literature there is a kind of comic grace in the ease with which he reaches his conclusion: "I sometimes catch myself thinking that in the future the role of literature will be close to that of a *sport*."

Before long one notices that Valéry rarely fails to plant such a key sentence at intervals in every sustained prose piece. Many of them have become famous. The opening sentence of the opening essay in his first collection, *Variété*, stirred controversy for years: "We later civilizations now know that we too are mortal." The two lapidary sentences italicized in the speech to the surgeons (*Il est possible de donner la mort*. It is possible to cause death. *Tantôt je pense et tantôt je suis.* At one moment I think; at another I am) pick up the emphatic rhythm of the two I have already mentioned: *Le feu tue* (Gunfire kills). *Le doute mène à la forme.* Valéry tells us that his poem, *La Jeune Parque*, took shape around a wordless rhythm sounding in his head; he speaks elsewhere of the *vers donné* or "given line" which becomes the armature of an entire poem. I believe these italicized sentences work in a similar fashion in his prose. In the dizzy spaces of thought a distant light shines forth toward which one can sight and slowly make one's way. A single thought, a profound platitude, or a verbal formula is enough. Then the rest of the essay comes together around that spark. One could, of course, take the contrary position and argue that these startling simplicities are not what he started with as isolated markers in the wilderness, but are rather the final results of the pressure of thinking patiently applied to anything whatsoever.

But in either case we are led to a related question that particularly concerns the "occasional" writer. Did Valéry have something like a method, a sequence of mental steps to which he could submit any raw material and produce a presentable written result? Frequently he leaves precisely that impression. Gide asserted that nothing Valéry wrote could be neglected. I remember hearing one of my teachers long ago state—apropos of which author I cannot recall— that "his mind was incapable of producing anything second-rate." It could be said of Valéry except at his most dutifully formal. He never ceased searching out the central command post of all thought. By 1924—give or take a year or two— he had organized his ideas, found a method of work, and discovered that he could turn his mind to any subject without wasting his time. Of course the external circumstances of his career thrust this responsibility upon him in great part.

His most seminal essays—"Introduction to the Method of Leonardo da Vinci," "Conquest by Method"—were twenty years behind him; their titles are not without significance. His debut as a public figure required that he be prepared to speak on all topics. It turned out to be possible, even rewarding. He already had a profound intellectual faith in the act of attention, and from the very earliest of his writings on Leonardo he had expressed a belief in the relationship between all things and all events. Given that attitude, he did have a kind of method or process.

Valéry's "method" had the effect of reducing the infinite variety of his subject matter to three themes: the mind, language, and everything else. His earliest metaphors for mind (a theater; a smoke ring) depict its turbulent equilibrium as circular and self-beholding. As time goes on he rejects with increasing vehemence any theory of separable mental faculties and portrays consciousness as a rhythm. His conjectures about a man hypnotized by the mere possibility of suicide relate directly to his description of Marshal Foch's dispatch in "acting on" an idea and find their full working-out in the speech to the surgeons. Valéry must have startled them with his example. If I know or think too much about what I am doing, I cannot do it. And in a beautifully turned page he asks the learned doctors: how, since you know so much about the organic functioning of the reproductive organs, can you bring yourselves to make love? He suggests that the solution lies in the existence of an alternating rhythm of being: "Now I think, now I am." We cannot be everything at once. This functional rhythm had already been described in a pithy little essay called "The Aesthetic Infinite": "To justify the word *infinite* and give it a precise meaning, we need only recall that in the aesthetic order *satisfaction* revives *need, response* renews *demand, presence* generates *absence,* and *possession* gives rise to *desire.*"

In these most critical pronouncements about mind, Valéry falls back on the sexual metaphor, or rather on the erotic ritual with which man, more than any other animal, has sanctified the act of mere coupling. No one could miss the atmosphere saturated with erotic feelings in poems of the mind like "Les Pas," "L'Abeille," and above all *La Jeune Parque.* In his theoretical statements, Valéry contrasts the aesthetic realm of infinitely renewable pleasure with the practical realm, where satisfaction obeys the entropy principle and returns everything to zero.

But most important of all to Valéry and to us are two intermediate realms where pleasure and delight arise under circumstances of restraint and reticence, two realms where we come to the threshold both of ourselves and of another person. Those realms are love and language. They lead us to the most precious and fragile acts of mind and body that we can know.

IV

Valéry's reluctance to surrender his poems for publication reveals how he acted on his conviction that a work of art is a kind of necessary and revealing by-product. The mental process that produced it is the true locus of being and value. Nothing is ever finished. The work of art constitutes both a distillate and an excretion, the part which is purged in order to allow the process to continue without poisoning itself. To my knowledge Valéry never used that figure; I insist on its aptness nevertheless. We examine feces in order to determine the health of the organism that produced them. But the byproduct may take on a value of its own. The entire Western tradition that erects the work of art into an eternal object surpassing contingencies of time, place, and personal creation, defined by intrinsic aesthetic principles and providing a substitute immortality, is now brought into question. Valéry is frequently seen as the last great representative of that classic tradition, which began with the Greeks, reappeared forcefully in the Renaissance, and reached its extreme and fetishistic stage at the end of the nineteenth century in France. But in spite of his youthful associations with the decadent school and the extreme cult of art, Valéry never finally yielded to that form of civilized coprophilia. His works show a preoccupation with the role of the poet as universal thinker and a steady emphasis on life itself as the theater of art. The last classic poet had a clear idea of the perils of formalism: "Civilization sustains itself only by a certain barbarity."

Only now can we broach the great paradox that defines Valéry. He seems to have lived an upright, quiet life, secure in the bosom of his family and the solitude of his study. He did not perform his poetry in public; he appeared before audiences as a poet writing prose, as a member of the French Academy, or as a professor at the Collège de France. The erotic escapades of his later years provoked no particular scandal. The portrait left us is of a supreme anti-romantic. Yet this muted figure came to believe more strongly than the Surrealists that art invades life. He even conducted himself in a fashion that deserves the epithet: "action poet." Richard Howard pointed out in a book review how Valéry's comparison of the act of painting to a dance anticipates recent theories of action painting. But the comparison also belongs to Valéry's total aesthetic and places him further than we ever knew from art for art's sake. His personal notes for 1928 contain the following observations:

The doing means more to me than its object. It is the doing and the making in themselves which represent the achievement, as I see it, the object. Major point. For the thing, once made, immediately becomes someone else's act. It's the perfect case of Narcissus. . . . And I come out with this paradox: Nothing is more sterile than to produce. The tree does not grow while it forms its fruit.

Valéry's poetics, as he sketches its outlines in the inaugural lecture for the Collège de France, rests its foundations on the execution of acts. It is not surprising that the controlling metaphors of that magnificent piece of thinking are economics and politics: not the creation of eternal objects but an art (and science) of action. The rest follows. A poem worthy of the name is the compressed and fragmentary record of a segment of life lived through with energy and attention. An essay pursues possibilities of thought and breaks off short of conclusions. In both style and sense the last sentence of "A Personal View of Science" displays Valéry's stance: "Man is an adventure. . . ." In this context one understands full well Valéry's long fascination with dance—a doing and a growing of form that does not produce anything other than what it is in the process of becoming.

Now if there is any truth in what I have been saying, one further thing becomes clear. We systematically read Valéry in improper fashion. First we probably read his poems; they are, willy-nilly, works of art belonging to special systems of language and of the fiduciary values of culture. Then we read his essays and speeches in areas that concern us. These works are admirable achievements, significant in ways I hope I have pointed out. But as *acts* they finally mean less than his letters and journals and notebooks.

In order to watch Valéry's self in action must we necessarily go to the twenty-nine monumental volumes of his notebooks and the various collections of letters? I see no alternative. In one of the texts we are likely to read last if at all, a letter written in 1917 to Pierre Louÿs, Valéry struggles with the problem of how to make proper use of those notebooks, how to publish them without systematizing, classifying, separating, uprooting, and thus killing their contents. The only answer he found was negative: "avoid discursive order" (*ne pas écrire À LA SUITE*). But he found a definition: "Literature growing wild. If you pick it, it will die." This impeccable stylist and former devotee of "pure poetry" attached increasing and probably final value to the inchoate states of his writing—the fragment, the sketch, the detached observation that has not found and may never find its place in a finished "work." This was his barbarity.

Is there any significance in the fact that Valéry's closest personal friends and intellectual confidants for the crucial early decades of his career were André Gide and Pierre Louÿs, an avowed and aggressive homosexual and a proud philanderer?

We neutralize such facts by separating the artist from the man, by dividing the work from the life. Thus Proust spoke of the *autre moi* who wrote his novels and was not to be mistaken for the social self that showed up at chic receptions and gatherings of less repute. It is a form of this separation that Eliot criticizes—and trenchantly—when he takes Valéry's poetics to task in his introduction to *The Art of Poetry*. Eliot states that Valéry "provides us with no criterion of seriousness. He is deeply concerned with the problem of process, of how the poem is made, but not with the question of how it is related to the rest of life in such a way as to give the reader the shock of feeling that the poem has been to him, not merely an experience, but a serious experience." It's a superb point, but it misses Valéry. For him the work of art was not, as it was for Horace and Petrarch and Mallarmé, the supreme value. What was?

Another tradition in literary criticism, with which we have been familiar and uneasy since long before Sainte-Beuve, sets up the life and the work of an artist as if they necessarily reflect one another. They form a kind of echo chamber or mirror device in which we cannot deal with one without the other. In various degrees and with shifting emphasis, the Dandy, the Decadent, and the Surrealist proclaim this reciprocal relationship between art and life. Their life aspires to the privileged state of a work of art. Correspondingly, their art absorbs their life. Huysmans' *À rebours* tells precisely such a story in what has always struck me as a more "experimental" novel than anything Zola wrote. Where does this grafting process leave Valéry and his two friends? The question does not apply. Valéry himself supplies the reason.

Following a limited number of leads in literature and philosophy, devoting himself to science and language steadily enough to make most of his critics resentful, Valéry introduced a third term mediating between life and art. He sees conventional social behavior and works of art as the outermost aspects of our individual existence. Adjoining them, however, and also adjoining our innermost life, lies a neglected domain of *acts of the mind*—private writings, decisions about one's acts, preparatory stages of "creation," reflections on one's self—a domain that forms a third term and modifies the linear relationship between the original two. Valéry refers frequently to his jottings as a form of geometry, and also used the expression "algebra of acts" to refer to a painter's mode of sensibility as contrasted with both his life and his finished work. If life and art are two semi-independent variables, and not two easily related elements of biography, then Valéry's intermediate "acts of mind" suggest a form of infinitesimal calculus that seeks and reveals their relation. To that perpetually renewed relation he devotes more time and attention and attaches more human value than to either of the variables it links. Valéry's truest work, which appears on every page he wrote but more directly in his "wild" texts, is his exercise of this calculus of acts, a psycho-poetic reckoning of "changes of mental states." He liked to call it a "Geometry of Time" at the beginning of his career and (in an essay inspired by H. G. Wells' novel) developed his theory of the symbol as a "time machine" that fuses and embodies different states. Later it took the form of a fine discrimination between unconscious, subconscious, and subliminal—accompanied by a sturdy preference for the conscious mind.

Valéry is a myth, of whom and of which we remain incredibly ignorant. He did not want it thus, but the way we approach his writings has produced that effect. We tend to dismiss as irrelevant the two most important facts about him. He renounced the composition of poetry not once but twice, even though the first time he was highly esteemed by fellow poets and the second time he had earned a worldwide reputation as a poet; and secondly, he spent the greatest part of his time meditating over a morality and ontology of thought based not on art but on scientific and mathematical models. He believed profoundly in the unity of mental process in an individual; the mind is one and embodies no essential division between *l'esprit de géométrie* and *l'esprit de finesse*, between reason and imagination. With equal vehemence he rejected any external unity—any system of events or knowledge of them that could lay claim to the term *universe*. To laugh at the scientific pretensions of Valéry's thought and to admit one hundred pages of verse (out of a total production of over thirty thousand pages) as his true contribution to culture is to capitulate to our prejudices. This heir of the Symbolists was heretical to the point of sacrificing permanence to the immediate and transitory. The reader confronts not an eternal object but the scenario of an organic event. Though smiling, Valéry has weighed his words when he suggests that literature will increasingly take on the function of a sport. Not art as the supreme spiritual value or a new priesthood, nor as something purely decorative and purposeless. It is rather that art, competing with the real strengths and promise of science, will become a valuable exercise of mental acts, a process whose products are beside the point except as they improve, extend, and record the game. We can all play, and it brings great joy. Naturally, the real pros like Valéry are very rare. When they play it is worth watching, for to follow so powerful a performance is to participate. The truly active spectator will already know that, like artist and criminal, he is as much the effect as the cause of his works.

I

Reception Address to the French Academy

Gentlemen,

THE very first words one addresses to the Academy always have a special ring of truth. It is quite remarkable that a speech dictated by custom, a formal acknowledgment which could easily succumb to well-turned, empty compliments, should invariably induce in the speaker the selfsame feeling he utters, a state of pure and perfect sincerity. At this singular point in one's existence, when for a moment one stands facing this Company before becoming a part of it, all our reasons for being modest, which are so frequently torpid and submerged, come forcefully alive. We are moved to appraise ourselves more severely than did the Academy. We feel we are of no weight. Our works seem a mere pinch of dust; and here, on the edge of your gathering, deeply sensible of all I owe to your good favor, I cannot but take stock of myself and conclude that miracles do happen.

You have readily accorded me the high honor of occupying among you one of the seats which so many supremely gifted men have had to spend long years coveting, and not a few of the very greatest, and most deserving, have waited an entire lifetime in vain. I should not be human, gentlemen, if this inescapable reflection did not prompt me to compare, in some fashion, my own with the destiny of others. The past takes hold of the present and I feel hemmed in by ghosts I cannot fail to mention. The dead have but one last resort:

the living. Our thoughts are their only access to the light of day. They who have taught us so much, who seem to have bowed out for our sake and forfeited to us their advantages, ought by all rights to be reverently summoned to our memories and invited to drink a draught of life through our words. It is but just and natural that, at the present moment, my memories should beckon to me, that my mind should be, as it were, revisited by a host of deceased friends and masters whose encouragement and whose perceptions by degrees guided me to where I stand. To many of these deceased I am indebted for being the man, such as he is, whom you have found worthy of election; and to friendship, I owe nearly everything.

It will come as no surprise to you that I single out from among so many dear and respected absent ones, whose presence is so vivid to me, the charming and serious face of your beloved colleague, M. René Boylesve, one of several academicians who persuaded me that I ought to consider the prospect of joining you one day, and who, devising the present occasion for me, sought with evident success to persuade you to feel well disposed toward my candidacy.

When Boylesve and I were together we would often talk about our literary beginnings, comparing our very different recollections of the time when we first met. It so happens that in those days our green enthusiasms, our ideals, our exemplars, our fetishes and infatuations had differed rather widely, for Boylesve had always been cool and level-headed. In a spirit of friendship we would rehearse our former differences just as formerly we had, in much the same spirit, acknowledged them. In the end we would always make common cause, as people who are not getting any younger are wont to do, in nostalgia for our irrecoverable youth. Though

4

nothing could be more commonplace than bemoaning what is gone, never was it more reasonable to do so, for the era of our youth and vigor had vanished not as it usually does, by imperceptible degrees, but died a violent death; it can only be glimpsed beyond gigantic events. The world that reared us into life and thought is a world now in ashes. We live as best we can among its disordered ruins, ruins that are themselves incomplete, ruins that threaten ruin, placing us in oppressive and formidable circumstances where the fading image of our past seems sweeter and more charming than it would, if time in its imperceptible course had quietly stolen away some tens of years from us.

So violent was this upheaval and so relentless the pressure exerted on men's minds, that a new literature emerged which was radically different from its antecedents. Living in 1890 or thereabouts, one was surrounded by quite another and much simpler pattern of ideas and ambitions. The republic of letters, in every generation raising and brandishing its many divergent mirrors before the world, no longer has the same ways or the same temperament it once had. Then, the various persuasions and sects were more mutually exclusive than nowadays. A youth trying his hand at writing and at the outset losing his way, dazzled as he might well have been by contemporary works and ideas, still lost no time discerning which parties and doctrines were dividing up the present and vying for the future. Before long, in that intellectual amphitheatre whose tiers rise from obscurity to fame, he would have had no trouble deciding on which side his preferences lay. In those days every faction of literary politics had its headquarters and arsenal. There were still two banks to the Seine, and from these enemy emplacements came the tattle of salons and the clamor of cafés; certain studios bubbled over with a frothy mixture of all the arts. One garret even gained renown, and such was its fertility that it became the only garret in the world capable of giving birth to an Academy, which complements its elder so well that we ought, you will agree, gentlemen, to pay tribute in passing to its distinction and talent.

Categories have ceased to be as tidy as they were in the age of our innocence. Purposes and systems used to clash with greater precision. The entire literary population arranged itself in a few tribes, according to the naïve laws of opposites which pitted art against nature, the beautiful against the true, thought against life, the new against the old. Each of these tribes had its incontestable leader, by which I mean a leader whose authority was contested, if at all, by someone waving the same banner.

Naturalism carried the day under Emile Zola. Grouped round the august figure of Leconte de Lisle, the Parnassian poets practiced rhyming as a rigorous art. In the forefront stood a mixed group, both smiling and pensive, whose influence far surpassed its numbers: the philosophers or moralists, some with severe, even gloomy dispositions, others so fond of irony as to have made of it a universal method, judging, anatomizing, and scoffing at everything on earth as in heaven.

I believe that, of all these ideologues, critics, theoreticians, humanists bred on philosophy, history, and exegesis, invoking the great names of Renan and Taine, not one missed being elected to the Academy.

Zola, Leconte de Lisle, Taine, or Renan: with these few names one could take one's bearings in the tumult of doctrines and personalities. Herein lies the usefulness of great men. Just as famous names are posted at street corners to tell us where we are, so these stand as guideposts at the major crossroads and many intermediate points of our intellectual memory. Fame thus ceases to be inane; it serves some purpose if it takes on the nature of a symbol and a useful convention in the general mind.

But these victorious schools, these constellations of writers, as they approached their zenith, began to exhaust the energy that had enabled them to rise. Their virtues and arguments ran dry, since most virtues are combative: in winning they are lost. So far as our arguments are concerned, they are for the most part projectile weapons good only for a single throw. Once they had come into their own, Naturalism and Parnassus fell an easy prey to inertia; it was not apparent to them that the only way out of an apogee is down. No young man drawn to letters could doubt—it would have been to doubt himself—that all sorts of extraordinary innovations were brewing in the brightest heads of his generation. Youth is a natural prophet, being what will one day be.

The intellectual air began to vibrate audibly with voices diverse and surprising, singing songs hitherto unheard, with the murmur of a deeply mysterious forest whose whisperings, echoes, and occasionally menacing or portentous gibberings seemed to distress or at least to mock at the reigning powers who, little by little, became secretly persuaded of their imminent downfall. At an age when we ourselves have barely begun to exist we are uncannily aware of the gaps and flaws in what exists already. A throng of short-lived publications, strange lampoons, pamphlets whose contents were startling to the eye, the ear, the mind, appeared and disappeared. Groups were born, died, were reborn, merged or split, testifying to the oceanic vitality submerged in the literature-to-be. I shall not pretend that the pleasure of behaving unconventionally, sometimes with intent to shock, did not motivate some among us. It was a role we assumed quite readily, that of the literary demon hard at work in his dark haunts tormenting the vernacular tongue, torturing the poetic line, ripping off its lovely rhymes and capital letters, stretching it to inordinate lengths, corrupting its orderly ways, making it drunk on unwonted mixtures of sound.

But, however severely we have been indicted in the past for our assaults, for our strange depredations, it should be borne in mind that we could not have acted otherwise. Men are compelled by circumstances to invent whatever they invent. Denunciations are so many expedients counter-ing other expedients. They are delivered by judges who cannot know our feelings from the inside. Severity is necessarily shallow.

How could we help but be pervaded by the spirit of our age, rich as it was in discoveries, bold in its undertakings, an age which has seen science translated into a tool, and seen the descriptive or contemplative attitude yield to the will to power, the creation of mighty means of action. It is an age that consistently flies in the face of man's observances and has, within a few years, transformed his ways and revised his sensibilities. It requires that we continually adapt our-selves, and we do, to new realities which, with a rapidity and thoroughness by now familiar to us, affect every phase of our lives, our status in time and space no less than our tastes and projects. What takes place one day in some obscure laboratory will, by the next, have had repercussions throughout the human economy.

No tradition could survive this riot of innovations unless by some stratagem. An age that leaves nothing unquestioned, that lives for experiments and sees room for improvement everywhere, that cannot but view everything as provisional and of provisional value—such an age does not make for stability in the arts and letters. The mentality that strives to make improvements does not strive for perfection. Improvement is one thing, perfection quite another. Moreover, altering the face of a page of writing is no great feat when the entire earth and whole cities are undergoing such extraordinary and radical changes.

Romanticism had already thoroughly stirred up the intellectual world, but the romantic rebel shaped himself in the movement of political violence that characterized the nineteenth century; something of the heat and dramatic frenzy of our revolutions rubbed off on his bearing and language. There was a hue and cry for freedom in the various forms and expressions of art.

The young people whom I knew, on the other hand, or at least those who had something in their souls to risk and to probe, were given rather to the kind of enthusiasm for experimenting, to the appetite for well thought-out innovations, daring solutions, and combinations that have made our science and technique what they are: great and phenomenal tools whose creations eclipse those of the imagination which, envious of these concrete marvels, has begun increasingly to look to them for inspiration.

Unavoidably the boldest experiments had to be tried, and any vestiges of the traditional or the conventional in art had to come under pitilessly close scrutiny. The chief concern in our quarter was to restore the natural laws of the music of poetry, isolating poetry itself from all elements foreign to its essence, gaining a more precise idea of the artistic means and possibilities at our disposal through a

9

fresh consideration and study of vocabulary, syntax, prosody, and imagery. Not all of us followed this line of thought, some preferring to trust their sensibilities, whose dictates they elaborated ad infinitum; but together we formed a literary movement more wracked by philosophy, more curious about science, more given to reasoning, yet more deeply animated by a mystical passion for knowledge and beauty than any other in the annals of French literature. It was inevitable that investigations so odd and, withal, so bold should produce difficult or disconcerting works.

This had the remarkable effect of creating a deep rift within cultivated society. Between patrons of the kind of beauty that puts up no resistance and lovers of another kind of beauty whose favors are given only if they are won; between those who conceived of literature as an art providing immediate enjoyment and those who sought above all some exquisite and intense expression of their souls and of the world, to be garnered at any price, a kind of abyss opened up, but an abyss bridged by mutual scoffing and taunts: the sort of signals everyone understands. The adepts were decried, laughed at. Opposition arose to the idea of an essentially arcane poetry. Its followers were dubbed initiates, and they found this designation to their liking.

Some had forgotten but others would have had the presence of mind to answer that all human fermentations, all schools and even the world's great religions have always begun as tiny coteries, cells long closed and impenetrable, proud to be flouted, and hoarding their private visions. At the heart of these secret societies new ideas would survive their delicate infancy, growing from germ into a body of thought. Friendship, sympathy, and certain feelings held in common, the unhampered exchange of hopes and discoveries, the recognition in one another of a kindred point of view the stronger for being shared, and, in some instances, mutual admiration: all these are the rare and perhaps elementary conditions for any intellectual resurgence. These little chapels where minds expand, these enclosures where the tone grows heated, and values inflated, serve as real laboratories for literature. There can be no doubt, gentlemen, that the public as a whole has every right to the regular and proven products of literary industry; but industry, to advance, must frequently be willing to grope, to make daring hypotheses, and even carry daring to a fault; and only laboratories can provide the intense heat, the extremely rare reactions, the degree of enthusiasm without which the sciences and the arts would be relegated to an all too predictable future.

Such were our literary coteries in that day and age. The young man that I was some forty years ago, under the spell of our pure and maligned poets and yet wavering at the threshold of their disturbing literature, which he heard denounced on all sides as mad and fraught with danger, sensed in the air of his time the same excitement, the same emotional state that charges a concert hall as the orchestra tunes up, each instrument seeking the note for itself and singing out, as it were, alone. It is a musical commotion delighting the soul it pierces, a chaos of hopes, an innocent state that is inherently short-lived; yet this living turmoil has something more universal, perhaps more philosophical about it than any symphony conceivable, incorporating as it does all conceivable symphonies, or suggestions of them all. It combines in its single presence the multiple future. It prophesies.

Intoxicated, shaken by these many promises, the budding poet grew amenable to the peculiarities of his age, allowing himself, like Parsifal—motionless yet moving—to be charmed into the boundless temple of Symbolism.

Meanwhile those wise and staunch divinities who see to it that our literature never deteriorates in some sudden and definitive way nor dozes for long out of sheer boredom with its own perfection had already formed and decked with laurel the very man needed to salvage, from the confusion of different idioms, some few of those graces once common among our purest authors. They had in no way suffered from prolonged disuse. Their revival came as a relief to a public half expecting some such event, and the man responsible for it swiftly and easily advanced to the front rank of his literary generation, distinguishing himself by a great adroitness in the time-honored devices of art, by a kind of caution or restraint rare, even bold, in an age given to impulsive ventures whose charm and merit he keenly perceived, gentlemen, though not so keenly as he did their weaknesses, their excesses, and their shortcomings. Without anyone's knowing when it came about, he acquired the aura and prestige of a classic, among all the aiders and abettors of a scandalously fresh beauty that found in him its most polished antagonist.

The public could not thank my illustrious predecessor enough for giving them water in the desert. By contrast with the highly complex and explosive styles being developed on all sides, the measured cadences of his writing proved mildly and agreeably surprising. It was as though fluency, clarity, and simplicity, the patron goddesses of the average man, had returned to earth. Those who prefer the sort of writing that gives them pleasure without requiring much thought took an immediate fancy to his work, whose seductive charm lay in its totally unaffected appearance, whose limpidity sometimes allowed a deeper thought, but nothing to mystify; his work remains, however, unfailingly readable, if not always wholly reassuring. He perfected the art of brushing lightly over the most serious ideas and problems. Nothing in his books gives the least difficulty unless it be the wonder itself of encountering none.

What could be more precious than the delectable illusion, created by such clarity, that we are enriching ourselves with ease, deriving pleasure without pain, comprehending without giving our attention, enjoying a free show?

Blessed are those writers who relieve us of the burden of thought and who dextrously weave a luminous veil over the complexity of things. Alas, gentlemen, there are others, whose existence must be deplored, who have elected to strike out in the opposite direction. They have placed toil of the mind in the way of its pleasures. They offer us riddles. Such creatures are inhuman.

Your great colleague, gentlemen, being less naïve about man, did not have this exaggerated confidence in the virtues of his reader, in his zeal and patience. Moreover, his courtesy was such that the ideas he dared to utter were never un-accompanied by the smile that withdrew them. There were good reasons why his elegance did not in any way impair his renown, which, as you know, soared to prodigious heights within a very few years. It soon became apparent that this renown, so inconspicuously acquired, had made him one of the most famous men of his time, and it was difficult not to admire this bantering genius for playing his way into parity with the reigning giants of European letters. He succeeded in adding to the massive and often brutal works of these men, so powerful in their time—the Tolstoys, the Zolas, the Ibsens—the leaven of his own works, in which he was content to ruffle dangerously what the others seized and shook with all their might, namely, the structure of our society and its customs.

I do not pretend, gentlemen, that it lies within my competence to give you an adequate portrayal of so considerable a man, having seen him only once, briefly, whereas most of you still carry a vivid image of him in your minds.

More than likely I shall miss the truth about him as a person and even as an artist. You must sense, moreover, how unequal I feel to the role of replacing a talent such as his, and how brazen in attempting this portrait of him. When it became clear that I would have to prepare such a eulogy, I realized what a formidable task was facing me. "What a splendid subject!" people exclaimed, which made me reflect that one can founder on even the most admirable reef.

Though a eulogy, gentlemen, draws its essence only from the flower of a man's life, and though it must not belabor the truth it advances, the act of writing it is necessarily animated by a strong and almost solemn sense of justice.

Even as we deliberate over the words we are to utter here about the man whose chair we inherit, we cannot help but feel tormented by the particular judgment we must pass on the deceased, weighing it on our conscience before we can isolate and arrange its finest conclusions and most admirable themes. We may indeed control the light that plays upon our model, but how are we to go about grasping the man himself? How does one form a clear idea of him? What basis have I for an equitable judgment of someone I never knew?

There is certainly no lack of records, opinions, witnesses. Everyone is talking at once. No sooner did the great man die than the image he sought to give of himself, disarmed of his living presence, began, like his flesh, to decay. Death leaves the dead man defenseless against the image of what he was. Reverential fears vanish. Tongues turn loose. Mischievous memories give vent to their anecdotes (which, you may be sure, are sufficiently savory); they swarm over the character of the departed, devouring whatever merits or virtues they can manage to unearth. Nothing can be more falsifying to the truth than its fragments; each fragment implants itself within the mind and soon becomes a full-grown impostor. The mind of man being incapable of preserving the truth whole and entire, even those who claim to possess it are never so immune to rancor or delight in idle talk as to escape being either piously false or slanderously true.

It is not unheard of for a dead celebrity to become a prey to a school of dangerous friends and anecdotic demons who lecture us on his perishable part. It is the curse of great men, gentlemen, that their fame allots them a second death: they die first as men, then as great men. One would think that the chief consideration for some people was the fact that a man did not measure up to the popular image of himself, whereas what we should consider is something that affects all mankind: that he did contribute to our sense of the dignity of letters and the mind. We have to realize that men are men, so much so that, stripped bare, we would not dare look at one another—each of us, given our obvious equality of faults, dejectedly settling for his own, in silence.

Let us then, gentlemen, wait out the bickering that inevitably rages for a time around fresh graves: let us keep our eyes on the gold that sparkles beneath the ashes.

Through the manifold excellence of his works, the variety and astonishing range of his culture, the consummate freedom of his mind, your colleague rose from a modest situation to one of the most brilliant, his labors, talents, and destiny guiding him from the grayish dawn that lit his beginnings to the dazzling twilight of his later years.

While musing upon this existence, whose progress was so smooth, upon this career pursued so confidently, at a pace unhurried enough to allow for all sorts of diversions along the way, I could not help but compare the orchestration of such a life with a few of those that could have been lived only a long time ago when nearly all men of intellect and even of wit wore the cloth, their conservative and scholarly intelligence being virtue enough to secure, even for those of humble birth, admittance to the highest circles. Accomplished humanists, metaphysicians thinly veiled in theology, re-nowned students of Plato, Lucretius and Virgil, figures half literary, half voluptuary, devoutly artistic, and only philo-sophically of the priesthood, all became cardinals at last, and once established, surrounded themselves with the loveliest shards of pagan antiquity; they were singular and attractive figures belonging to an age that is no longer, when the Church could still tolerate prelates of exceeding refinement and incredible freedom of thought.

Our own age no longer provides the unusually gifted mind with the means to develop at its leisure, sheltered from the ordeals of life, in the shadow of some vast institution. Gone are the prebends and the abbeys. Leisure is no longer a part of dignity. On the contrary, our society, obsessed with precision and the tangible, is notable for its inability to find for the intellectually gifted man an appropriate and tolerable place in its gigantic and crude economy.

The situation was, if anything, worse when your col-league first appeared on the literary scene. The century proved unable to stop breeding literati and equally unable to find a means of supporting them. The bitterness that ensued! The sorrow! The toll of wasted lives, lives meant for the highest attainments, yet for that very reason rewarded with destitution and the most menial tasks! Things came to such a pass that diplomas were guarantees of misfortune and vouchers of distress. Jules Vallès, Alphonse Daudet have left us frank and frightful accounts of these literate hardships. Scores of young men were trained only in those disciplines which destined them to unemployment; young paupers were brought up to the most useless attainments. They learned, the hard way, that the most knowledgeable elements in any society are also its most expendable. Emerging from adolescence, the future creator of Jean Servien might have observed this plight all around him and entertained legitimate fears that it might become his own. He might have dreaded the fate of a Vingtras or a Petit Chose. But he was too versatile, too rich in general knowledge and, besides, too well-versed in the facts of life not to assume almost instinctively, almost without thinking, the identity he would have one day. His philosophy, which was his very nature, protected him, moreover, from hard and fast resolutions at one extreme and from premature resignation at the other. He would not commit his future. He would not tie himself to a definite profession, or to any literary school. And if one day he did allow himself to be bound, it was with the most pleasing of bonds.

Essential to his inner life, then, was its flexibility and many-sidedness. It allowed for the spiritual and the sensual, for moments of detachment and of desire, for a curiosity huge and ardent but traversed by deep prejudices, a certain complaisance born of passivity but a reflective passivity, the passivity of great readers, which is hard to distinguish from study, a surface passivity not unlike the stillness of some liqueur with too much body, forming perfect crystals in its repose. It was not with impunity that he acquired so much knowledge, so many ideas, for at times, without always meaning to, he would startle, scandalize people with tastes less various than his. He was fertile in doctrines that contradicted one another in his mind. He would fix only upon those things he found beautiful or piquant, and his only permanent convictions were artistic ones. His habits, his thoughts, his opinions, his political views fell into place within an elaborately harmonious whole that did not fail to astonish and sometimes to puzzle. But what sort of mind is it that does not have contradictory thoughts, that does not place its power to think above any one of its thoughts? The mind that does not baffle itself, does not abandon verdicts it has just reached, routing them with its own weapons, does not deserve the name of mind. Only if he possesses a wealth of conflicting ideas or what we believe to be so, does a man amount to something in the realm of the intellect. So coarsely do we express our perceptions of other people that, as soon as we are confronted by someone of greater scope and freedom than ourselves, our attempt to describe him gets lost in contradictory words and we end up attributing to a human being some monstrous nature, born of our own feeble expressions.

This enormous capacity for contradictory qualities is something we ought, rather, to admire. We must give our attention to the curious phenomenon that, indolent by nature, he was an insatiable reader who somehow produced a considerable body of work; a man sensually inclined who could steel himself to the boredom of an unremitting task, a waverer, mincing his way through life as it were, who, once he had overcome his initial modesty, rose to the top by indecisive steps; a stammerer who could bring himself to make, sometimes violently, the most daring pronouncements; a man of intellect, and subtle intellect, who could learn to live with the public's simplified image of him, and to wear the rather garish suits of fame; the soul of moderation and temperance, he nonetheless took sides, with great and astonishing vigor, in the main issues of his age; a man of fastidious tastes, he was reputed a friend of the people and, moreover, actually was one at heart.

I am fully aware of the gossip. People have not refrained from whispering—or even from roundly asserting—that because they seemed foreign to his easygoing and careless nature, his more active qualities were really owing to someone's tender and insistent will, to an imperious presence who made her cause the advancement of his fame, standing long vigil over his work, animating, and, so it is said, protecting his mind lest it dissipate itself in the pleasures of society, who persuaded him to draw out of himself all the treasures he might otherwise never have known he possessed or else might have neglected from day to day, renouncing them for the delight of enjoying the beauties to be found in libraries and museums. But even if this were true, even if it could be proved that much of his work might have remained unwritten without the gentle insistence of her affectionate discipline, only malice could derive some advantage from knowing this.

Only very rare talents have the gift of arousing in others such a strong protective instinct, such energetic affection, so sustained a zeal for works yet to be, and so profound a sense that they must be urged into existence. Is it then of no account, to have won the kind of strict and absolute devotion that hopes, in the end, for no higher reward than the satisfaction of having served to fulfill a brilliant destiny?

Thus, gentlemen, we must fix our attention on the work as it stands.

This work does exist, and survives. Its merits are as clear as its substance. Everyone knows, everyone appreciates the virtues of his art, whose consummate grace achieves an effect of exquisite simplicity.

But here we come upon a singular circumstance in the fortunes of his work, the fact that, with all the dignified beauty of its chaste form, it won not only a high reputation, as you know, but a popular one. This is almost unbelievable. It has no precedent in modern literature, where one must always anticipate, as a matter of course, that only those books in which content swallows form, and effects do not depend on the delicacy of the means, will receive popular acclaim.

Any explanation for this sort of phenomenon would undoubtedly have to be sought in the virtues of our language which so skillful a writer as he so deeply grasped and handled so lightly. He demonstrated that it was still possible in our language to convey a sense of the wealth inherent in a long-continuing culture and to combine the legacies of admirable writers who had followed one another in an unbroken line. Our great writers, gentlemen, are not great solitaries as they frequently are elsewhere, but then France has what other countries do not, an atmosphere favorable to literature, especially so, as it proved, in your colleague's case.

He himself could have been possible and even conceivable only in France, whose name he adopted as his own. Under this name, not an easy one to bear, which only a man flushed with hope would have dared adopt, he won favor with the entire world, though undeniably he showed the world what it preferred to see, a France wholly embodied in its comely appearance, pleasing without ever giving cause for embarrassment or worry. The world would not be unwilling to have us serve a purely ornamental function; it would put up with us as the jewel of the earth. It would allow us, rather generously, to represent the happy few, in an otherwise crass age, who worship exquisite things, and to pass for a nation of artists and patrons, content with their lot, their heaven, their abundantly beautiful land, forgetting all the blood we have lately shed, the evidence we have given of persistent energy, of unshakable and indomitable will, our collective readiness to perform sacrifices, our ability to muster vast resources while besieged on every side, as though all this, our recent history, did not give us the right to address the most overweening powers with absolute poise, directness, and even authority.

But it is a rather different France which her famous homonym portrayed with such elegance, a gentle, refined, desultory France, a France somewhat weary and seemingly disenchanted, and he captured her image perfectly from that deceptive angle. His own mind was a highly composite emanation of the France he knew. Numerous traditions long since developed and dissipated, revolutions political and ethical, a whole store of contradictory experiences had gone into the making of a mind so encyclopedic and so indecisive. A creature of such freedom as that would seem like the latest born of some ancient and almost collapsing civilization, a born collector of all the beautiful things men have made and preserved. He had long inhaled from books the fragrance of life past, pervaded with an odor of death, and his spirit, redistilling what history had distilled of itself, became gradually imbued with this refined essence of past centuries. We can picture him in the garden of French culture, leaning over the most scented, the rarest—or sometimes simply the wildest—of flowers; culling his favorite bouquets and trimming his hedges; a great gardener for whom grafting and pruning held no secrets. Thus nourished on honey, flitting through the vast treasuries of history and archaeology much as he fitted through those of literature, without spurning the comforts, the conveniences, the diverse freedoms of his own age, the plaudits of the public and of women, resorting whenever he needed them to the diversions of society, yet not allowing himself to be so lulled by all these advantages and delights as to overlook contradictions, and to let fools go unscathed, he composed, at his leisure, books whose continual charms belie a rather sinister view of the world lurking underneath. Moreover, he knew how to live well.

In no sense was my famous predecessor an innocent. It did not seem likely to him that sometime in the future humanity would be substantially different from what it has apparently always been, or that man's zeal and his quest for the absolute could one day work untold miracles. He did not possess invincible faith in the advantages of the mind, but through his wide and intimate knowledge of all that is readable, and much that is not, from the past, he had made himself independent as it were of the present and the future.

He was born in books, reared in books, forever athirst for more books. He was versed in all the aspects of a book— paper, type, format, binding—and knew whatever was known of its printer, its author, its editions, its sources, its fate. During his lifetime he was in turn a bookseller, a librarian, a judge of books, an author. He was, to the core, a man of books.

I must say, gentlemen, that the mere thought of all those immense stacks of printed pages mounting throughout the world is enough to shake the stoutest heart. There is nothing more likely to confuse and unbalance the mind than scanning the gilt-lined walls of a huge library, no sight could be more painful to the mind than those shoals of volumes, those parapets of intellectual produce that rise along the quais, the millions of tomes and pamphlets foundered on the bank of the Seine like waste, abandoned there by the stream of time thus purging itself of our thoughts. One's heart falters in the face of so many works—even, indeed, so many master-pieces. The idea of writing resembles the idea of adding to infinity—it leaves a taste of ashes on the lips.

In this valley of Jehoshaphat, confronted with such a multitude, even the rarest genius finds his peers, and is indistinguishable among the hordes of his imitators, pre-cursors, and disciples. Every innovation dissolves in the mass of novelties. Every illusion of being original is swiftly dispelled. At the thought of these myriad creatures armed with pens, these innumerable agents of the mind, the soul darkens with mixed feelings of sorrow and the irony of profound pity, for each one fancied himself, in his hour, an independent creator, a first cause, a sole owner of truth, a unique and incomparable source, only to end in the common pit, lost beneath an ever-growing mass of others like him, having labored all his life and consumed his strength to earn immortal distinction. Under the weight of this crushing presence, all is leveled out; nothing survives the unbearable company it is obliged to keep: no thesis is without its antithesis, no affirmation goes unrefuted, no anomaly re-mains singular, no invention but is rendered obsolescent by another and obsolete by the next, as though some impersonal process were at work making our language yield every possible combination of its syllables, and as though, in the end, the actions of this host of free and autonomous beings were like the functionings of a machine.

Your learned and subtle colleague, gentlemen, did not feel this unease in the face of great numbers. He had a stronger head. Unlike those who are subject to statistical vertigo and revulsion, he did not need to take the precaution of reading very little. Far from being oppressed, he was stimulated by all this wealth, freely drawing upon it to direct and sustain his own art, with happy results.

More than one critic has taken him to task rather harshly, and naïvely, for being so knowledgeable and for not being unaware of what he knew. What was he supposed to do? What did he do that had not always been done? Nothing is newer than the standard of absolute newness imposed as an obligation on writers. It requires truly great and intrepid humility nowadays to dare be inspired by others, but this is rather less in evidence than a spirit of constraint, a fastidious craving for priority and, by and large, a certain affectation of virginity which is at times something less than delectable. Neither Virgil, nor Racine, nor Shakespeare, nor Pascal took pains to conceal the fact that he had read. But disdaining current opinion and giving this small matter closer scrutiny, we can easily clarify it; it is not at all a matter of aesthetics but, if anything, one of ethics, for it involves vanity. Only because these two ideas have been confused has such discredit fallen on the ancient and respectable custom of combining mine and thine.

A book is an instrument of pleasure, or at least aspires to be one. The reader's pleasure is wholly unrelated to the trouble we have taken making the book for him, just as, when offered some rare dish, I do not fret over the delicately prepared meat because someone other than the chef may have invented the recipe. What do I care about its inventor? Least of all do I care about the pains he took. I do not dine upon his name and I do not savor his pride. What I am consuming is a moment of perfection. To think otherwise would require nothing less than looking at the world through the eyes of a god, for gods may presume to pass judgment on merit, but we humans have, fortunately, a quite imperfect understanding of merit. The very notion of merit calls for an extremely bold metaphysic; it leads us to hypothesize, in some measure, the ability to be a first cause which we then, going beyond hypothesis, ascribe to someone.

Moreover, our mode of reasoning in such difficult and lofty matters as these is so frivolous that, showing a singular disregard for logic, we confer the highest dignity on authors whom we call inspired. We believe them to be the pure instruments of some afflatus outside themselves, indeed, beyond the whole of nature; we turn them into oracular reeds, thus granting them both the glory of prime merit and the immense privileges of irresponsibility.

Far from espousing current superstition, gentlemen, I find good grounds for admiring someone who is able to choose, who does not pretend that he is oblivious to our heritage of beauty, whose discriminating knowledge of the treasures amassed by time allows him to recapture the means by which such perfection was achieved. The mystery of choice is no less a mystery than that of invention, assuming that the two are quite distinct. Furthermore, we have absolutely no idea what lies at the bottom of the one or the other.

Coupling this gift of choice with its prodigious learning, the gardener of Epicurus' Garden could not help but reveal in everything he created a mind keenly aware of all the magical resources of language and the intimate presence of the purest and most beautiful models of our art. They were the furnishings of his powerful memory. He felt completely at home with all in our language that is most sonorous, graceful, limpid; and he was equally alert to the ways in which it shows how trenchant, how destructive, how quick-witted and redoubtable, how exquisitely damning it can be. His novels, which are not so much novels as chronicles of a world he openly reviled at the slightest provocation, are written in a tone of classic irony that was his natural, almost instinctive manner of expressing himself; so sustained is it that those rare passages in which he lays aside his smile seem written by someone else, as though for the moment he were not being serious.

It must be owned that the society of his age, which survives in the midst of our own, offered to the satirist a wealth of material. Within and around himself he found a conglomeration of extremely dubious ideas and circumstances which could easily provoke the most skeptical judgments.

I am convinced, gentlemen, that a civilization's age must be computed by the number of contradictions it contains, by the number of irreconcilable customs and beliefs that confront and qualify one another, by the multiplicity of philosophies and aesthetics that so frequently live together in a single head. Does this not describe our own predicament? Does not each of us abound in different notions and biases that are blind to one another? Do we not find that every family now contains a variety of religious persuasions, or races, or political views, as each individual contains a whole armory of internal dissensions? Modern man (and it is in this sense that he is modern) lives on familiar terms with a host of contraries which have taken root in the penumbra of his intellect.

I should observe here that tolerance, freedom of opinion and of belief, always appears quite late in the life of a civilization; the idea becomes conceivable, and pervades laws and customs, only after minds have been progressively enriched and softened through the exchange of their differences.

At the same time, these mental organisms, because of the inherited cultural incongruities bound up in their substance, become dangerously unstable compounds. A single incident might explode any of those deep contradictions lying at their base, inert and dormant but easily detonated. Remember this, gentlemen! Now, let us promptly forget it!

It was enough for the author of *Contemporary History* to become aware of how incoherent the state of things was, and he was confirmed in that skepticism which earned him so much reproof.

It is difficult to corner a skeptic. He has only to confront us with our own curiously ambiguous attitudes toward doubt. We prescribe it in the sciences; we require it in business. Yet suddenly we will point out its limits and disqualify it as we choose.

We forget that every doctrine trains and urges us to damage or demolish every other. We implore those who make comparisons not to do so, not to push their arguments to a logical conclusion when in fact the latter move and evolve of their own accord in our minds. We do not care to notice that doubt derives from things themselves. It is, intrinsically, a natural phenomenon, an involuntary reaction that protects both matter and mind against intolerable images, as we see very clearly in the case of a sleeping person whose dreams are so absurd that, even in the absence of reason, this absurdity is enough to evoke a marvelous resistance, a response, a negation, an emancipating act, an awakening that flings him out of an impossible world, restores him to the realm of probability, and, at the same time, provides him with a kind of physical and instinctive definition of absurdity.

Thus it is not so much the skeptic we must indict as the cause and occasion of his doubt, the flimsiness of what he touches and knocks over; and also the inevitable sense of comparison that arises whenever we bring together what we know.

A man distinguished for his inordinate eagerness to know everything was bound to have a skeptical and satirical cast of mind. His immense learning gave him abundant powers of disenchantment; he could easily make any social observance appear mythical and barbarous. To his erudite and ingenious mind, our most respectable customs, our most sacred beliefs, our worthiest ornaments seemed suitable stuff for an anthropological collection, along with the taboos, the talismans, the amulets of primitive tribes, the cheap finery and artifacts of outworn civilizations fallen to the power of curiosity. In such collections and vestiges, the spirit of satire finds its most vulnerable targets. There is not a doctrine, not an institution, not a society or a regime that does not bear the onus of some uncomfortable memory, some undeniable fault or error or embarrassing variation or even, in some cases, inglorious origins, beginnings founded on an unjust act which, in the interest of its latter-day grandeur and pretensions, it would prefer to forget.

Laws, customs, institutions—these are the common and

cherished prey of critics of the human species. The persecution of these substantial and imperfect entities is merely a game, but played so unremittingly through the ages as to have become a tradition. It is pleasant, easy, at times perilous, to belabor them with irony. Indeed, certain souls find nothing more intoxicating than to respect nothing. The writer who dispenses such pleasures to the lovers of his wit allows them to share his own pitiless lucidity and gives them the delicious sensation of being like gods, above good and evil.

The eternal victims of this free and learned mind might have answered, by their mere existence, that were it not for them the world would enjoy precious little freedom and no learning whatever. Freedom and learning are scarcely products of nature. What little of either that men possess they have labored to acquire and used cunning to preserve. Nature is not liberal, and gives us no reason to suppose that it is concerned in the least with the welfare of the mind. On the contrary, mind must struggle against her to assert itself. Men band together to thwart their destiny, chance, the unforeseen, which are things they can never cease to reckon with. What is more natural than chance, and what more unquestionable than the unforeseen?

In short, order is an immense, anti-natural edifice whose parts may be criticized only if the whole remains intact, protecting, sustaining, sheltering its critics, furnishing them with the leisure, the security, and the knowledge they need in order to criticize.

Literature itself requires a whole system of conventions superimposed on those of language.

It is precisely here, in the domain of letters, that our thinker seems, at first glance, to have behaved inconsistently.

The dogmas, the formal laws he treated with such scant

respect when they obtained in the world of morality and politics, are the very idols he consulted when arranging and consolidating his fictions. He esteemed above all other master-pieces those that observe the strictest rules of poetry.

It is common knowledge that he nurtured a veritable passion for Racine.

How Monsieur Racine would have responded to this zealous admirer of his we shall never know, but it might be amusing to imagine a meeting between the Jansenist courtier and the doubting libertarian. I thought for a moment, gentlemen, of arranging a dialogue between these Shades for your benefit, but for fear they might find themselves hopelessly at odds (not to say, exchanging the most cutting remarks) I have left them to rest in peace.

In the one, quite fortuitous, interview I was privileged to have with our great student of Racine, Racine was our one topic of discussion. I was far from imagining that within not so long a time it would be my office to eulogize your colleague, so I was not moved to ask what he would have me say about him here in this chapel, which I never dreamed I should enter. I was filled with apprehension. I sensed that there were quite a few subjects that might bare our differences. I might be tempted to voice certain long-standing grievances. In his prime he had been a critic, and an out-standing one in terms of style and knowledge, if somewhat less so in prescience. He was not one to put his hope in things that might possibly come to be, nor in things newly born, nor one to attune his highly sensitive ear to the sound of grass growing. Such desires sometimes bring on hallu-cinations of the ear. . . .

May his Shade forgive me for saying so, but he was not very eager to prophesy. He did not believe in prophets and so he did not obtain the gift of prophecy. At most, he was a "prophet of the past."

In certain passages of *The Literary Life* he showed no great lenience toward the young poets who were just beginning to test themselves, nor toward their chosen masters. He never conceived any great hope for them. He declared that he felt no connection whatever with them, and expected they would amount to very little. Sometimes he compared them to ascetics, which, even coming from him, was after all more or less bearable. But at other times, he found little to choose between them and Hottentots. He wrote that beautiful things are born painlessly, which was not good advice; it is the sort of advice that produces Hottentots. Yet it is true that on other occasions he also declared the opposite.

This exceedingly intelligent man could not and would not bother to ask himself why and how an appreciable number of young people understood and loved what he himself could not fathom.

I have often said to myself, gentlemen, that if criticism had the magical power to abolish what it condemns, if its edicts, carried out to the letter, could do away with everything it considers harmful or deplorable, literature would suffer a sorry fate. Erase the existence of all the hermetic poets, the heresiarchs, the demoniacs; remove the euphuists, the lycanthropes and the grotesques; submerge all the dark, Byronic souls in everlasting night, purge the past of all its literary monsters, defend the future from them, and admit only the craftsmen, desiring nothing more than their miracles of balance, and I predict, gentlemen, that the great tree of our Letters will promptly waste away; even the very art that you admire, and with such good reason, will gradually perish.

But, to come back to this interview of ours, we talked about Racine, great resource that he is—Racine, whom he admired more faithfully, scrupulously, usefully above any other author; Racine, whom he worshiped and read as a very different person, Joseph de Maistre, had done in another age; Racine, whom I, too, have admired in my way.

I admired him as best I could, having discovered him at thirty years' remove from the schoolroom and when I was engaged on some of those tiny yet immense problems that beset the working poet. This incomparable craftsman had seemed to me, when I was young, nothing more than a product of the school education which in those days happily forbore from teaching us to love. I do not regret that long misappreciation, nor belated appreciation. Never do we assess a man's greatness more accurately than in having to compare our weaknesses with his strength. If circumstances set us a hard task, similar to one he has performed, we marvel that he could untie the knot, could surmount the obstacle, and so, in our own helplessness, we have the best and most precise measure of his triumphant powers.

An hour slipped by unnoticed in that only conversation. As I was about to withdraw, my future predecessor payed me a compliment. He said that I had spoken well on Racine, and so I left pleased with him, that is, with myself. I do not remember what fine point he was gracious enough to allow that I had made. All I had done, probably, was to express in my own way the thoughts common to all who delight in music and are moved by perfection. I am quite certain that I praised that astonishing economy peculiar to Racine's art, which atones for the sparse means at its disposal by possessing them so completely. Few people clearly understand how great an imagination is required of the artist who would do without imagery and strive for so stringent an ideal as Racine's. It is, no doubt, true in the sciences as in literature that an image may at times replace some more difficult turn of thought. Racine preferred to work it out. I see him in the first place drafting, then defining, and at last deducing from some thought long held and turned over in his mind, those immaculate periods of his, in which even violence sings, and the intensest and truest passion rings clear and golden, and never deploys itself but in the noble tones of a language that consummately weds analysis and harmony.

To enjoy it fully, one must understand Racine's deep-seated reasons for rejecting those effects that came into vogue after him, the absence of which in his work has often been a source of reproach. Any one of his lines that seems empty to us was retained at the expense of twenty more sumptuous versions which would, however, have broken a sublime curve and disturbed the august suspension of some perfect phase in the movement of the soul.

After I left the little house where I had been so graciously received, the questions we had discussed continued to trouble my thought.

During these states of intellectual resonance that follow and prolong a meaningful conversation, the ideas we have talked about but have not exhausted continue to form every possible combination in our minds.

For a time our thoughts quicken, enlarge as it were their sphere of play, throw light on things within us that we had never suspected, whereupon we come to ourselves again; we return, that is, to a state of minimal consciousness.

The dialogue that had just ended now resumed within my mind, transformed into an exchange of hypotheses, each more daring than the last. The mind thus set in motion and left to its own devices will stop at nothing. It automatically generates bold ideas that spur one another on.

I began to reflect on the peculiarity of that art we call classical, and observed that it begins to appear as soon as man's accumulated experience becomes a factor in the composition and appraisal of works. It is inseparable from the notion of precepts, rules, and models. . . .

Presently I came to ask myself why this art was promulgated and, more especially, why it prevailed in France. France, I reflected, is the only country in modern times where form is held in high repute, where there is a demand and a concern for form in itself. Neither the power of ideas, nor interest in the description of passions, nor the miraculous formation of images, nor even the outbursts of genius are enough to satisfy a nation so fastidious that its likes must await confirmation from its intellect. It is not willing to distinguish between what is written spontaneously and what is to be read reflectively. Only after it has found good and universal reasons to admire will it unreservedly admire, and the search for such reasons led it, in a previous age, to make a careful distinction, as the ancients had done long before, between the art of expression and what is actually expressed.

It is not surprising (I thought, still absorbed in my musings) that this distinction should have gained ascendancy in a country rather disposed to doubt. The sense of form and the cult of form, it then seemed to me, could be understood as passions of the mind, born of the mind's resistance. *Doubt leads to form* was, in brief, my conclusion.

Reflecting then upon the man I had just left, and his love of classical art, for which he was known almost as much as for his extreme professions of skepticism (he was doubt personified), I began to suspect some secret but highly attractive relationship between the cult of form and the critical, skeptical turn of mind.

Credulity, I thought, is not difficult. It is its nature not to be. It asks only to be ravished. It allows itself to be abducted by impressions, mirages, and, since it exists entirely in the moment, it tells of surprises, wonders, enormities, of the strange and the miraculous. But there comes a time, though not in everyone's life, when mind at its most detached begets its own corrective. Just as doctrines and philosophies that offer themselves without proof find it increasingly difficult as time goes on to elicit belief and, instead, grow more and more controversial, until finally only the verifiable is held to be true, so is it in the realm of the arts. Scientific and philosophical doubt finds a kind of literary counterpart.

But how are works to be protected against the repeals of reflection and buttressed against the feeling that they are arbitrary? By means of the arbitrary itself, but the arbitrary organized and decreed. Skeptics creative in their own way have established conventions as a systematic defense against personal deviations, against superabundance and confusion, and, above all, against unrestrained fantasy. Conventions are arbitrary, or at least present themselves as such; but there is no room for skepticism where the rules of a game are concerned.

What I have said may appall you. To imply that classical art is an art whose guiding ideal is something like that of a game—such is its self-awareness, its success in accommodating both rigor and freedom—is no doubt shocking; but your shock will, I trust, subside after a moment, in only the time it takes to recall that perfection, in human terms, consists and can only consist in exactly fulfilling a certain expectation we have established for ourselves.

Classical art says to the poet: thou shalt not make sacrifice to idols, whose beauty resides in details. Thou shalt pare thy vocabulary for there are certain words, the rare and baroque, that draw all attention to themselves and glitter vainly at the expense of thy thought. Thou shalt not seek cheap effects nor shalt thou speculate on the exotic. Thou shalt not attempt to strike down with awe, for thou art not a god, though thou mayest think so. Do only this, if it is within thy power: convey to men the idea of a perfection that is human.

Classical art says many other things besides, but to explain them there are spokesmen more learned than I. I shall be satisfied to repeat briefly what is generally said of that art: it is astonishing that it should have been the privilege of one country, France, under the dominion of free intelligence, to create an art the epitome of grace, an art whose extraordinary constraint flowered into a superior ease of style, a fluent intimacy between form and thought, a delectable discretion.

Let us consider further how this was brought about. The shackles of the Muses were cruelly reinforced, their steps numbered and their natural movements fearfully hampered. The poet was chained, encumbered with weird prohibitions laid upon him for no apparent reason. His vocabulary was decimated. The laws of prosody became tyrannical.

Once these strict and often absurd conventions had been promulgated, something happened, gentlemen, that to this day fills us with wonder: through the activities of half a dozen consummately gifted men and the grace of some few salons, miracles of purity and of measured power and life were born and bred, incorruptible works that make us bow, despite ourselves, before their faultless countenances; like goddesses they attain a degree of naturalness surpassing nature.

Gentlemen, I do not offer you these deductions of my imagination as solid or profound thoughts. This is but an arrangement of ideas that I could have wished otherwise. I should have liked to portray more skillfully the multiple faces of my famous predecessor, and display more felicitously those great qualities of his that entitle him to the attention of posterity.

A mind charming and nimble to a fault, the passionate lover of whatever was most beautiful in every literary genre and, withal, a friend of mankind, he will be remembered in the history of letters as one who demonstrated afresh the remarkable relationship subsisting—as I have tried to show—between independence of thought, the purest and most rigorous system of art ever conceived, and our free and creative nation in itself.

In Honor of Émile Verhaeren

Gentlemen,

I HAVE been asked by the French Academy to act on its behalf in paying homage to the glorious memory of Émile Verhaeren.

We welcome this occasion to greet Belgium's Royal Academy of French Language and Literature, represented here by our eminent colleague, M. Henry Carton de Wiart. A scant few days have passed since the mortal remains of the Poet were interred in the village of his birth, Saint-Amand, on the banks of Flanders' great river, in accordance with Verhaeren's own wishes. He felt almost filial affection for the Escaut, a tenderness so great that in one of his poems he expressed the hope that one day his body would be buried in the earth of its banks so as to feel, in death itself, the nearness of its living waters.

Today our own river greets his image. Paris has given this bronze a place near the Seine. It could not have been allotted a more auspicious site. On the river nearby, barges pass slowly along, wearing their distinctive colors as they arrive from Flanders by canal. From aboard one of the docked barges, a tawny dog barks at people walking to and fro along the quais; rosy-cheeked children with pale hair are running about playing, heedless of the gigantic city; and through tiny windows framed by starched, well-ironed, and divided curtains one can see something of the tidy little rooms behind, so impeccably arranged that they seem enclaves of domestic Belgium here in the heart of Paris. Thus, between this corner of the capital, happily chosen to receive the effigy of the great poet, and the plot he himself chose as his final resting-place, there is a living and continuous connection of waterways.

Moreover, the monument we are unveiling today stands in the very shadow of that ancient and charming church, Saint-Séverin, which one admirable writer, a Parisian of Flemish stock and Flemish name, Joris Karl Huysmans, loved so well, whose stones and whose soul he so fondly and curiously cherished. The two will make harmonious neighbors here. Between their ways of seeing and feeling there is an obvious affinity which extends, remarkably, to their similarly nervous and radical temperaments. I can easily cite, in passing, at least one peculiarity that I observed in both Huysmans and Verhaeren, a feature common to both these men who, for all I know, never met during their lifetimes.

Both of them showed an invincible aversion to the brilliance and fixity of azure skies. Huysmans as well as Verhaeren detested that absolute and sustained splendor of the heavens which is the glory of southern lands. Both were afflicted with the same intolerance for blue skies and were equally partial to the "misty suns" and "humid heavens" celebrated by Baudelaire, and even to those "blessed fogs that muffle our brains" of which Mallarmé speaks in a marvelous prose poem.

Verhaeren carried his love of damp weather to imprudent extremes.

Once I met him as he was returning from Italy. With horror he described its implacably blue sky. Florence and the crushing limpidity had driven him away; as the train bringing him back to grey atmosphere was approaching Dijon, clouds began to gather overhead, at last; presently rain began to fall. Verhaeren was so elated, so filled with a sense of well-being that he could not resist opening the door and, at the risk of his life, stood on the steps of his carriage in order to feel, if only for a few seconds, the blessed shower. But France, gentlemen, was able to offer him a wide variety of climates. It has its sunny lands and its misty valleys. In its art, as in its nature, it possesses the wonderful gift of reconciling fog and azure.

It willingly provides a common ground for strongly divergent views and expressions, for by custom it welcomes and understands.

This, perhaps, is why—more than any other nation in modern times—it has lured so many writers of different ethnic origins to practice its language.

The wealth of our literature fascinates and attracts antithetical minds, natures that defy comparison, from every part of the globe. I pity those who complain of this.

As for myself, gentlemen, I am perpetually amazed that, during the same period, in the same quarter of a century, French poetry could enrich itself with great works as important, but dissimilar, as those of Jean Moréas and of Émile Verhaeren. I have no desire to attempt a comparison of their poetics.

Indeed, there is no possible basis of comparison between the followers of Apollo and the companions of Dionysus. Their lines shall join at infinity.

If Greece presents us with a pure, grave statue and Flanders offers us Memling and Rubens, what could be simpler than to accept such different tributes, though we do so with mixed feelings of gratitude and pride: these gifts, taken together, bear witness magnificently to the universal esteem in which our culture is held.

Think, gentlemen, of the great gifts that Flanders has made us in the past forty years—a brilliant group of writers, singularly vigorous and colorful, some of whom have gained worldwide renown.

Georges Rodenbach, Charles Van Lerberghe, Maurice Maeterlinck, as well as Émile Verhaeren—each obeying his genius, and all obeying the genius of their race—have increased our literary fund with noble and precious works—ranging from the profound to the delicate, from the odd to the earthy—that will, by their scope, remain in our language as representatives of the Flemish character, whose traits are unmistakable and whose paradoxes are fundamental to it.

We now possess, in French, some splendid products of this race, which is distinguished for its odd blend of impetuosity and langor, violent activity and contemplative leanings; it is a race at once ardent and long-suffering, sensual to the point of frenzy yet, at times, wholly detached from the sensible world, enclosed in mystical castles which the soul secretly builds for itself on the border of intelligence and night.

I shall never forget, gentlemen, how impressed I was when I first read Maurice Maeterlinck's preface to his translation of Ruysbroeck the Admirable. To me that slender volume seemed to contain the essence of an entire culture, hitherto wrapped in mystery but for occasional glimmerings imparted by the masters of Ghent and Bruges in their paintings. Émile Verhaeren, however, opens our eyes to something else again: the world of acts and bodies. Verhaeren's powers, in order to exert themselves, needed the colorful, busy, vibrant universe.

Not that he was, at the beginning of his career, and until

the middle of his life, unacquainted with the lower depths of melancholy; he had lived psychic centuries in anguish and sorrow, and at times had even been on the verge of despair.

I believe that there are few poets who do not go through a fundamental crisis between the ages of twenty and thirty, one in which the destiny of their gift is at stake. A crisis, that is, a trial between contending forces, an inevitably tragic confrontation of ambitions, abilities, ideals, memories, and presentiments—in short, a battle waged by all the elements of contradiction, all the antagonistic themes which a life (already long enough, experienced enough to have accumulated them) propounds to the torn soul and foists their conflict upon the ravaged organism.

This trial shook Émile Verhaeren to the depths of his mind and body, for its violence and inherent dangers depend on the greatness of the soul affected, and on the nobility of its preoccupations. It is not the common lot to endow eternal riddles with infinite value, or to find cause in oneself to suffer hideously on account of conceptual problems. From this fearful struggle, Verhaeren emerged victorious, a great poet, and his own creator.

Gentlemen, if only we could observe with a metaphysical eye the underlying organization of the mind and perceive the secret workings of mental life—how it is formed, gropes after itself, discovers itself, and becomes an identity, how it disengages itself from events and takes increasingly definite shape—an artist's existence would then appear, I am certain, as a long and constant preparation for some sovereign state of being: we should be privy to the making of a creator.

This spectacle would teach us that the paramount work of an artist is his own self—the individual instances of his handiwork, his completed and palpable creations being the mere means, the outward effects of that self, and often the result of some accident.

Thus the artist—his self's major achievement, its unique and hidden work—comes into being by small degrees, construes and recognizes himself; he becomes a new man, one who does what, ultimately, he alone is capable of doing.

In this way was Émile Verhaeren, emerging from his long crisis, reborn. He triumphed; he returned from the hell of his own heart and mind bearing the terrifying remains of that enemy he had slain in himself.

Three books, three strange witnesses to the great torment, unburdened him of the atrocious moments he had lived through: *Les Soirs* (*Evenings*), *Les Débâcles* (*The Debacles*), and *Flambeaux Noirs* (*Black Torches*).

You know what a dynamic poet was to emerge from this. He swept from his path whatever might hinder the full expansion of his poetic genius. He rid himself of all problems whose source was not within himself alone. He sacrificed some of his primitive qualities, decimated his desires, rejected his secondary talents the better to possess his essential kingdom, the domain of his real freedom. The time had come when he could emerge in his greatest power and clarity of outline.

This kingdom, this domain which he made his own, belongs properly speaking to life itself, such as it is lived in our age. Until his advent, poetry had barely touched upon the subjects which life today, mechanical and brutal, mighty yet enslaved, offers to man's astonishment, to his horror, his wrath, and his hope. Modern man has placed his grandeur outside himself. Minute particle though he is of the world that includes and will survive him, he has striven for a century to transform the whole by artificial means; and we

43

have scarcely begun this immense project, whose limits and consequences cannot be foreseen.

Yet, by his memories, his instincts, his most tender and inward promptings, man still belongs to the natural world, the world that once was virgin and spontaneous in all its phenomena.

Thus, man is at odds with himself, mighty and wretched, unequal to his triumph, and very like a stranger in this new estate and manor he has built with his own hands, the product of his own inquiries, of his calculations, and his inflexible will to understand and rule.

Gentlemen, we are living a great drama. This drama has found its voice. The themes of our life, divided as it is between what was and what is becoming, this spectacle of nature overturned and of men's frenzied impetus, has found in Verhaeren its impresario, its master, its incomparable singer. Through him, our materialistic civilization has been given the high dignity of lyric expression. Verhaeren's enthusiasm and rhythm sanctify the toil of towns black with smoke, the imposing or extraordinary façades reared, developed and multiplied through the prodigious exertions of industry. The thought of factories, of huge ports, of dynamos, of the frenzied and conglomerate activity of men and machines was enough to transport him. His poems seem at times to be directed toward an apotheosis of energy and the power of fire.

But his great heart could not be fulfilled by any such inhuman delirium. Verhaeren felt endless pity, admiration and love for our race, enslaved by its own devices, imprisoned in huge cities that seem to draw, suck in and consume people! He gave a name to these monsters whose weird life feeds upon human substance: *tentacular* creatures whose rampantly growing and alarmingly active body, with its chaos of inner relationships, and whose incessant production of ideas, vices, luxury, political and artistic sensibility require ever more fuel in the form of people, of living and thinking substance which they absorb and transform ceaselessly.

Today Verhaeren compels universal admiration. He is at the height of literary glory. His name is familiar to everyone who reads poetry. His works are being translated abroad, and in many lands they have even found a popular audience. But his destiny is not yet complete. Within his own nature he had, so far as he was concerned, fulfilled himself. His task was done. He could be well content with the balance between his mind and its creation, and could afford to rest upon the gifts he had bestowed.

But he was to receive, from life as he saw it, something totally unexpected. Who could have foreseen what, in time, the force of circumstances would make of him? War broke out, and the formidable events that ensued have increased the greatness of a great poet, investing him with the highest honors, or, more precisely, the highest function a poet can perform.

In the normal course of things, a poet, however illustrious, is but an ornament of his country. He is a sumptuary creature, a luxury whose existence merely signifies the determination of some few people to express, in language quite distinct from the vernacular, what is purest in the domain of least useful thought.

Yet it sometimes happens that a people overcome by misfortune, with even their very hearths violated, bereft of their independence and sensing the imminent danger of losing their existence as a nation, will discover in the poet—in that otiose gentleman who used to sing of their customs and traditions, who exalted and reflected his country, giving it fame and immortality—a necessary man, a man whose works can serve as a symbol of their existence and a vehicle for their hopes.

What a plight was Belgium's during the war, gentlemen! History offers no parallel. Never has a nation been so cruelly and clinically dismembered. There was a line of fire, a frontier of ruins, of cadavers, a barricade of death; and to one side of this appalling line lay the territory of Belgium, subjugated by an enemy power, answerable to the harsh law of the conqueror, its people deprived of all semblance of free-dom, sovereignty, political character, their unity threatened and their very awareness of being a people slyly under-mined.

On the other side, beyond the trenches, and as though in some other, inaccessible world, the King, the Government, the Parliament, and the Army were assembled, acting, working, waging war on foreign soil.

Man had never beheld anything comparable to this: on this side the State and on that the People, and, between them, the insurmountable rage of war.

But this people enchained, a people brought to their knees and at the same time being urged to forfeit their soul, these Flemings and Walloons could, in the midst of their misfortune, captive and wanting national direction, invoke the venerated name of their poet, of the great Flemish poet of the French language.

Just as Dante once meant *Italy* to the scattered Italians, Verhaeren became the name of a national deity in the mind of oppressed Belgians. It was a magnificent and, in a sense, a total career, Verhaeren's: suffering, energy, lyric power, and profound love of mankind vouchsafed him, the most human of men, fame as a hero of his country. To the glory of the creator he was finally to add the glory of the servant.

Reply to Marshal Pétain's Reception Address
to the French Academy

Sir,

UPON THE DEATH of the great Foch, there was no doubt whatever either among the public or ourselves as to who ought here to take the place of such a leader.

In our own minds you were already elected before you could even have thought of presenting yourself to us as a candidate.

Your immense services to France; merits of the most substantial order crowned with the highest dignities; the confidence you inspired in the troops, and that of the nation which has kept you at the head of its forces in times of peace, all this pointed you out for the chair left vacant by the great commander—even that contrast, doubtless most auspicious for the successful outcome of the war, which marked your character, your conceptions, and your methods of carrying them into practice.

No one could have rendered more accurately the praises of Marshal Foch, or described to us his works and acts with more clarity, precision, and firsthand knowledge than you were in a position to do.

That, sir, is what you have just accomplished. From your lips, we have been listening to reason analyzing imagination, firmness controlling fire, calm measuring the storm; and a splendid tactician, a consummate craftsman in the art of force, has given us a masterly outline of how the plans and enterprises of that impetuous poet of forceful strategy were developed.

We have listened to you with an attention particularly sharpened not only by the fact of your personality, and the great theme of your speech, but also by certain circumstances for which we cannot help feeling some regret.

That war, though still so close, and still so much with us, is nevertheless imperfectly understood in some of its particulars. There are aspects that grow obscure as we look at them; verdicts once simple shade off into doubts, and indefinable confusions and uncertainties of opinion have arisen. What was done, and what might have been done; the real motives for decisions taken; individual roles in the achievement of victory; all this is brought under renewed discussion, and we find we are assisting at the painful birth-pangs of what the truth will be, we are sorely divided witnesses of history as it laboriously takes form. It is, in a sense, the future of the past that is in question, and is being put in dispute, even among the great shades. Those who were at one and revered each other in peril, now become eternal adversaries. The illustrious dead give voice, and the words from the tomb are bitter.

But you, sir, fortified by that great, that almost legendary calm which attests its confidence in what will endure; sustained by that watchful common sense which distinguishes you, by that prudence and foresight which have made you the Sage of the Army; you who keep, as a frontier to your thoughts, a silence which we feel to be fortified with facts, solidly organized in depth, you at least are that rare man whom the severest critics, the harshest controversialists, the very ones who ceaselessly practice the role of belittling the famous, and whose chosen vocation is to damage any greatness impressed on the public mind, have been obliged more or less to spare. Even politics—which thrives on injustice—appears to respect you.

It is because of your cool and clear approach, your reticence, your abstemiousness in promises and soothing predictions, your fixed determination to accept reality, keep to the fact and pronounce it at all risks, that people have kept their bounds with regard to you, and that you have been able to remain unmoved, without fear of belated revelations, re-examination of your actions, and the inquest into events. All your commands are there, awaiting history. History will find in them models of the greatest precision, views that were always clearcut, exhortations that were always simple and humane, orders that were due, fair, and feasible, conceived and drawn up as they were by a leader who could have carried them out as though they were imposed on himself. But you were chary of putting too much petty detail into your injunctions: the wisest of your precepts has been to leave to each man, in all grades of command and in all the specialized tasks of an army the responsibility for what is peculiar to his rank and calling.

In every case, your aim was to be understood by all, each man having to work out according to his own lights the part of your plan which fell to him. Your critical and ironical cast of mind, judging others by itself, shrank from demanding a blind or conventional trust which you yourself would not have conceded. You chose to inspire hope by acts of foresight, a positive preparedness, rather than to rouse it with speeches. During an ordeal so prolonged that at times it seemed endless, words day by day lost more and more of their face value. But you were seen to be controlling practical tasks, organizing and reorganizing your units, taking care of the feeding, the resting, and the morale of your troops; and above all, so possessed with the importance of how plans worked out in the execution that you were constantly revising and renewing the training of troops and cadres, exercise and combat each profiting the other, your thoughts always dominated by practical experience. Your actions speak, and your words are actions.

Thus, from rank to rank, in the groping heart of an unprecedented war, you never ceased from your will to procure, between opinion and action, between the idea, the means and the men, a kind of harmony or interdependence, without which you felt there was no continuity of advantage and no resource against reverses.

A servant ever ready to serve, expert in all that pertains to war, within a few months you reveal your ability to command an immense army as clearsightedly as you would a division; but fully capable, thanks to your character, of accepting a division after commanding an army; which proves both a complete mastery of your craft and a prime force of personality, for only such a personality could accommodate to every post and take its mastery along with it.

That was how your promotion became inevitable. You are he among our leaders who set out to war with six thousand men and ended it at the head of an army of three million.

What did you do? To mention only the two greatest things, you saved Verdun, and you saved the soul of our army.

How did you achieve this? What do these signal services imply in you?

The salvation of Verdun, the sudden and miraculous renewal of the spirit of our troops, these were not—they could not be—among the inspired acts, the high deeds that result from a lightning flash of intellect or energy, the happy chances seized and exploited to transform a situation in a moment, and at once resolve the destiny of an army. The time for such prodigies is past. In a war that is geared to slowness, where the most brilliant coup can only be deadened in a matter of days against the masses and resources of great and powerful nations totally organized for the struggle, inspired to all-out resistance—lightning strokes, genius, sublime solutions cannot avail to wipe out the opponent.

I do not know if you foresaw this, but it was in your nature to do so. Happily, you among all were one of those who are most apt in themselves and best prepared by their instinctive cast of thought, to grasp—or rather, not to refuse to grasp—the stationary, the in a sense retardatory character of a total war, conditioned by an indefinitely prolonged balance of forces and deepseated resistances. The creed of attack pure and simple had never won your allegiance. You had no love for inflexible theories. You kept always in mind that the real is made up of a quite irregular infinity of particular cases, whose nature must be continually subject to fresh analysis; and you took action, against the enemy at Verdun, against the internal crisis in 1917, by way of methods individually thought out and precisely adapted to the danger and the given circumstances of the moment. You did not, in those terrible conjunctures, improvise either the admirable tactical judgment or the profound knowledge of men which were the basis of success in each case.

Your hard-won triumphs were the effects, the long-ripened fruits of a lifetime of reflection, dominated by a truly scientific care for precision as to the evidence and prudence in your deductions.

The greatest trials could inflict no change on this impeccable method of approach. In you there was no case of a new man's being brought to birth by the war. You were content to let experience inform the mind that was ready for it, and it was enough for you to remain he who had learned once and for all that the true value of an intelligence consists in the ability to be taught by events.

That, sir, is why I can rightly say that nothing reveals you in a truer light than your finest achievements. In them all your everyday qualities show up. In them all that you had acquired since youth, not from schooling but from personal experience, was put to work. And first among these qualities I discern one essential insight, into the soldier.

At the outset of your career, as a lieutenant on the Alpine frontier, you lead the very same life as your riflemen in their mountain maneuvers. You know how to get on with them; you build up a true picture, to be invaluable one day, of the French soldier, who is so little like the soldiers of other countries. You note his easily won disposition, his hatred of condescension and of those constraints which seem to him purely arbitrary, the self-esteem which prompts him to any exploit offered him as a challenge, and the deep-seated reasonableness whereby he moderates his impulsive nature. It is hard for him to tolerate the feeling of useless effort. Doubtless there are demands which cannot always be explained, duties whose purpose is of long term, circumstances where passivity must be imposed. But it is not the part of a true leader merely to dictate orders without any concern for their effects on men's minds: such orders would only meet with a corpse-like submission. It must often be the case that a troop of men is worth exactly what it thinks of its leaders.

Our soldier has the singular fault of wanting to understand. Ours have always been armies of individuals, with all the good and bad consequences that flow from such a state of things. No use trying to obtain from a lively and critical people that formal discipline, that rigid bearing, that perfection of timing and rhythm which are so impressive on parade. Automatism was never the strong point of our armies. It can be invaluable in war; or it can prove fatal if the leaders have lost their heads, or their lives.

The future—if we may be permitted to invent it for a moment—could be sufficiently in our favor granting the hypothesis that military power would rest much less on the sheer size of the effective forces and the weight of numbers, than on the personal value, the boldness and mental adaptability of the individual soldier. The airman, the machine-gunner already give us an idea of what the human agents of conflict might be like. The new weapons tend to wipe out indiscriminately all life within a larger and larger area. Every concentration becomes dangerous, every assemblage draws fire. No doubt we will see develop small groups of men, acting as chosen teams, bringing about overwhelming results in a few seconds, at a fixed hour, at points unforeseen. This is what may happen, and it will add incalculable weight to the qualities of the individual.

But we are not yet arrived at such an advanced era. We see you in command of a platoon, or a company, in some peaceful garrison village. I can well imagine you in such a command. You know all your men by name—which is anyhow a duty—and I am certain you know a good deal of their lives and characters. If I have said that the French soldier likes to understand, he likes equally to be understood. As a result the relations between officers and men in France are more human and therefore more interesting than elsewhere. It is perhaps by way of this relationship between leaders and led, the greater or less degree of mutual understanding, mutual rapport, that national armies differ most from each other. A young Frenchman who spends several years as a subaltern can draw incomparable lessons from his experience. If he is observant, he can study the mingled lives of our national types in their great range and variety, he can watch how individuals of the most diverse shades of culture, fortune, and profession behave under the enforced equality of military life. To study the face of one's country territorially or on the map, is not enough; its men must be understood. Consider our history once more. . . . Truly, I can think of no profession more apt to ripen a sound understanding—supposing that quality always increased in us in proportion to the value of our opportunities.

Here then is how I like to imagine you, sir, in your peacetime career, shaping, thanks to the duties and privileges of your position, that real insight into the men in the ranks and their reactions, from which you will draw such useful applications many years later.

But the study of life in no way impeded your study of the most specialized sections of your craft. All the while you were carrying out the sufficiently monotonous duties of your place, leading the regulated and arduous life of an active officer which calls for so much faith and submission in order to carry out the as it were endless liturgical round of the soldier's year—receiving the new recruits, training them, shooting-practice, inspections, maneuvers—all this while, you were applying your mind to the working out of what seemed to you most positive and precise in the science of war. After a few years you had become a virtual authority on the technique of artillery fire.

You examine such problems with a clear and exacting eye. Other people's ideas seemed not to impress you greatly. Presently you make a discovery which, to a profane eye, would have appeared simply naïve. But we know, from the examples of science and philosophy, that what looks obvious to the ingenuous sometimes disappears to the eye of the masters, thanks to the very fixity and fineness of their concentration. Then it is that only a genius can perceive some essential and very simple truth, hitherto obscured by the studious labours of many thinking minds.

You discover simply this: *that gunfire kills. . . .*

I am not suggesting that this was until then unknown. Only there was an inclination to ignore the fact. How could this have come about? Simply because theories can never be elaborated without some cost to reality, and there is no domain where theories are more essential than in that of military strategy, where practice has to be imagined in order to establish precept.

It became clear to you that the prevailing tactical rules tended to give scant importance to this idea that *gunfire kills.* Their authors saw it chiefly as a matter of wasted bullets and time lost in wasting them. It was pretty well universally taught that firing retards offensives; that the man who fires must dive for cover; that the ideal thing would be to advance without firing; that no doubt a certain number of cartridges must be expended, but only to soothe the soldier's nerves. Firing was a sedative, prescribed reluctantly as a special concession. So this remarkable conclusion was arrived at: that the only function, not to say excuse, for firearms was their effect on the morale of those who used them. . . . As for the enemy, it was thanks to sudden approach, to the imminent threat of the shock of sheer numbers that the spirit of defeat was born in him and decisive victory won. *To conquer is to advance*, people would say. They might as well have said: *to conquer is to convince.*

History, which by its nature contains an example for everything, which provides support for every thesis, and arms all opinions with *facts*, offered the apostles of this tactic a generous supply of them. But you, sir, who could not but consider other matters besides the chaos of contradictory instructions which the past offers us, you saw clearly that in war, as in all things, the tremendous increase in the means of force tends to diminish more and more the physical contribution of human action. From this simple consideration one might make bold to assert that *every happening in history in which technology and machines played the least part can no longer serve in the future as a model or example for anything whatever. . . .*

Firing kills, you would say. . . . A modest proposition it seems now. It belongs to a time when the machinegun was not yet in its glory; it was still new and unappreciated, considered insufficiently *tough*, good at best for coping with the glacis and trenches of a military works, but apt to go astray in the field in clumsy hands, and apt to waste away in a few minutes the resources of a battalion. This was the common sense view. Common sense cost us dear. We live in a bewitched and paradoxical era which plays at falsifying the most sensible deductions. In fact, what turned out to be most indispensable in the last war, *in defiance of common sense*, was the fearfully effective introduction of more and more complicated mechanical material. The machinegun above all, though costly and not very *tough*, transformed potentialities, and decimated forecasts as it did men.

So it was putting it modestly to say that fire kills; fire today mows down, wipes out, arrests movement and life over any zone that it covers. Four determined men can hold back a thousand, can knock down dead or alive any who show themselves. Which leads to the surprising conclusion that the power of the weapon, its *yield*, increases with the numbers of the adversary. The more there are, the more it kills. That was how it got the better of movement, drove fighting into the earth under cover, impeded all maneuver and in a sense paralyzed all strategy.

Having made your discovery you could not but draw your conclusions. You work out a strategy of your own, very different from the one which was taught; and the forms in which you present it are directly opposed to the precepts that advocated unconditioned movement.

You sum up your conclusions in striking maxims: *an offensive is an advance of gunfire; a defensive is a halt imposed by gunfire*. And finally: *the cannon conquers; the infantry takes over*.

Forward movement accordingly ceases to be the heroic panacea. Man is no longer the supposedly irresistible projectile to be lavished without stint until victory or complete extinction; man's function is to complete the work of gunfire, and his advancing is no longer a cause but a consequence. You clearly saw that a new war required new tactics, whose main feature ought to be the early and massive application of cannon fire, engagement *at a great distance*—just as action at *any* distance will perhaps be the essential feature of wars to come.

But this, sir, gave you a point of view that can only be called *heretical*. The path of heresy, we must own, led you very high—to the very summit of your profession, to glory, and, finally, here, where the way of literary heresy also leads on occasion.

So openly did you collide with ideas that were then supreme that the orthodox tacticians of the Army might have held it against you. Such was hardly the case. In spite of the audacity of your views, and the dominance of a not very tolerant dogmatic school of thought, be it said to the honor of your chiefs that the freedom of your views—and their causticity—did not deter them from recognizing your talents and appointing you professor of tactics at the École Supérieure de la Guerre—that is at the very center where the theories you openly questioned were elaborated and taught.

I believe it was at this point that your career crossed for the first time with that of your illustrious predecessor. Foch, having become director of the School, left you entirely free to teach a doctrine he did not altogether share. I like this trait, which could only be that of a great man.

By this time your ideas were clearly fixed, your mental positions, your judgments solidly founded.

On the one hand a just and ever-present sense of the human element, a sense of its real resources which will always count in your calculations: real insight into the soldier given a capital place.

On the other hand, an exact idea of your experimental tactics, a clear-cut image of warfare adjusted to the demands of powerful armaments.

But combat is the common element of battle in general; practice is what keeps ideas in repair. If strategy chooses to ignore tactics, tactics can ruin strategy. The overall battle won on the map, is lost in detail on the terrain. Here as in all the arts—I might say as in all our acts, even the simplest— insight (which is foresight) and the act of carrying it out in practice can only have value through each other.

Ideas precisely worked out, knowledge slowly built up, clear and fixed conclusions—will you ever have the opportunity to put them to the proof?

Will war break out one day?

What a strange phase of History it was that might be called the era of the Armed Peace, and of which I would like to say, though I cannot, that it is now only a memory!

Throughout forty years, Europe is held in suspense before a conflict which people knew would be of unexampled extent and duration. Not a single nation is safe from being involved in it. Every man has his conscription papers by him. Only the date is missing. On some day unknown, the hazards of politics will see to that. For forty years the coming of spring was to be feared. The opening buds remind men of the season that favors war. The outbreak seems at times inconceivable; it is shown to be impossible. And the Armed Peace weighs so heavily on the nations, overloads budgets to such a point, imposes such obvious constraints on individuals at a time of increasing moral and political freedom, it clashes so obviously with the ever-increasing trade exchanges, the ubiquitous intermingling of interests, the international blending of fashions and pleasures, that to many minds it seems not altogether improbable that this paradoxical peace, this false equilibrium, should turn little by little into a genuine peace, unarmed, and above all freed from *ulterior motives*. It seems unbelievable that the edifice of European civilization, so rich in such a variety of interlocked interests, should ever be brutally torn apart and break out into a squabble of nations mad with rage.

Many a time did politics draw back from the payment of its account, well though it knew this to be the most likely result of its lethal activities, and its brutishly simple motive forces. Life, creation, prosperity even went on under the loaded sway of the Armed Peace, under the always imminent stroke of that notorious Next War which is to be the Last Judgment of the great powers and the definitive settlement of age-long quarrels and conflicts of interest. The whole picture, made up of a system of tensions, suspicions, and precautionary measures; a continually intensifying uneasiness, compounded of persistent causes of bitterness, inflexible pride, fierce competition, joined to the fear of imaginable horrors and consequences unimaginable; all this went to form an unstable yet durable equilibrium, at the mercy of a breath, and yet subsisting for nearly half a century.

Certainly there was, in Europe, a whole quantity of explosive situations. But the heart of this vast complex of dangers lay in the nature of Franco-German relations as created by the Treaty of Frankfurt. As a peace treaty this was a model of the kind that leaves a possible door open for war. It placed France beneath a latent threat which in the upshot left her only a choice between perpetual vassalage, barely disguised, and recourse to desperate measures.

As a result, between 1875 and 1914, on each side of the new frontier a symmetrical rivalry of armed force declared itself. The prelude to any history of the Great War must be the history of that peculiar war of safeguards and fears, the war of armaments, schools of thought, operational planning; the war of espionage, alliances, and agreements; a war of budgets, rail-tracks, and industries; a hidden yet never-ceasing war. On either side of the frontier—while cultural activity in the arts, sciences, and letters offers the brilliant spectacle of an ever more elaborate civilization, ever more remote from violence—there are men profoundly dedicated to their ruthless tasks, fully sensible of the frail foundations of this splendid edifice of peace, of the explosive inner charge of antagonisms and hatreds, men who at the critical hour will find themselves invested with tremendous powers and responsibilities, and who are preparing for the awful day which may never come. They work in secret, along the same lines. The high commands make calculations, their opposing plans cross and cancel each other, out-guessed, or exposed. They work out every hypothesis, find an answer to every improvement in the rival system, each striving to turn to its advantage some decisive inequality. On the two sides of the frontier, still invisible, remote indeed from the glory, the capital eminence which war will bring them, the von Klucks, the Falkenhayns, the Hindenburgs, the Ludendorffs over there; and here, the Joffres, the Castelnaus, the Fayolles, the Fochs, the Pétains, each according to his temperament, his race, his weapon, or his post, all are living in the future, awaiting destiny's orders.

Never in any era was there anything to compare with this long war, hidden and yet present, intense yet conjectural, a sort of hand-to-hand contest in technics and intellects, with its imaginary surprise attacks and retaliations, its new inventions of machines and methods, whose novelty at times upsets fashionable theories, modifies for a moment the balance of forces, breaks the course of routine.

A whole specialized literature—and a fantastic counterpart sometimes more accurate in prediction than its rival—offers the imagination a picture of the cataclysm to be, which Europe is big with. How weird, how utterly novel is this intense awareness, this prolonged and lucid vigilance!

The *War of Tomorrow* will not prove to be one of those catastrophes that no one dreamed of.

But on the two sides of the frontier there is a great difference in the conditions for the labors of preparation. All the weight is in Germany's favor; the essentially military form of government, its prestige based on victory; a growing population, naturally inured to discipline; a kind of racial mystique; and in many minds an implicit faith in might as the only scientific basis of right.

On our side, nothing to compare with all this. A national temperament at once critical and restrained; a population rate rather less than stable, in a country where life is easy and pleasant; politically a nation most divided; a government whose vice and virtue was its sensitivity to the slightest changes of opinion. Such conditions made it difficult for any methodical and sustained preparation for a war which no one wanted or could want; and which everyone, if he thought of it at all, could only imagine as an act of defense, a reply to aggression. One may say that the idea of declaring war on a neighbor nation has never occurred to the French mind since 1870. . . .

Nevertheless our Army, so often criticized, exposed now to suspicion and now to political temptations, reduced to inner turmoil on certain occasions, was able, in spite of all these difficulties, to carry through immense tasks. Some mistakes were made; but after all we must not forget that the Army's errors and its virtues are our own. It is inseparable from the nation it reflects. The country can see its image in its shield.

You were just about to leave that Army, sir, to quit the career that had called to your youth and filled up your life; about to enjoy the melancholy charms of retirement, since you were fifty-eight years old, when the hour struck. The Archduke's blood had flowed. The last moments of peace had come.

But the carefree nations were enjoying a season of splendor. Never was the sky clearer, life more desirable, or happiness more ripe. Perhaps a dozen important personages were exchanging telegrams or visits. That was their business. The rest had their minds on the sea, hunting, country life.

Suddenly, between the living and the sun, passes an inconceivable cloud of mortal chillness. A universal anguish takes birth. Everything changes color and value. The impossible, the incredible is in the very air. No one can fixedly and individually consider what exists, and what is to happen next alters as if by magic. Everywhere the reign of violent death comes in by decree. The living rush about, separate, re-form; Europe, in a few hours disorganized, reorganized, transformed, equipped, drawn up for war, enters fully armed on the unforeseen.

On the other side, the war is welcomed in general as a full-scale operation, needed in order to break up a troublesome system of hostile nations, and to open up new possibilities of expansion for a tremendously prosperous empire. A huge confidence prevails. It seems impossible that so much preparation, so much material and such a will to victory cannot overcome all resistance. The war will be brief. Peace will be dictated in Paris within six weeks. The sky washed clear by the necessary storm; Europe amazed, daunted and disciplined; England put in her place; America arrested in her progress; Russia and the Far East dominated. . . . What prospects, and what opportunities! And remember that nothing of all this was quite impossible, that these apparently preposterous aims might well prove reasonable.

As for us . . . But is there any need to recall our supremely, simple reaction? For us it was simply a question of to be or no more to be. We knew too well the fate in store. We had often enough been told that we were a decadent people, breeding fewer children, losing faith in ourselves, going to pieces pleasurably enough on the land we had enjoyed for too long.

But this enervated people was also a mysterious one, logical in reasoning, but surprising in its acts.

"*War?*" said France. "*So be it.*"

And then came the most poignant, the most significant, and let us say the most reverend moment in her history. Never had France—simultaneously struck by a single light-ning flash, revealed, restored to herself—never had she known, never could she know such an intimation of her inmost unity. Our nation, the most diverse and the most divided of nations, appears as *one* to every Frenchman in that same instant. Our dissensions vanish, and we wake up from the monstrous images we had made of each other. Parties, clans, creeds, all the widely discordant notions we had formed of past or future, become one. All is resolved into pure France. For a time was born a kind of unforeseen friendship, a universal and sacred intimacy, a strange and quite new gentleness, resembling that of some initiation rite. Many were amazed in their hearts at loving their country to this degree; and just as a sudden pain can waken us to a deeper sense of our bodies, and light up for us a reality by its nature unseen, so the thunderstruck awareness of war made all see and recognize the real presence of this Fatherland, that inexpressible thing, impossible coldly to define, not to be determined by race, language, land, interests, or even by history; something which analysis can deny, but which thereby resembles, as it does by its overwhelming potency, passionate love, faith, or one of those mysterious states of possession which lead man to where he did not think he could go—to a point beyond himself. The feeling for Fatherland is perhaps in the nature of a pain, a rare and peculiar sensation by which, in 1914, we saw the coldest minds, the freest, the most philosophical, seized and overwhelmed.

And yet, among us this national feeling blends easily with the sense of humanity. Every Frenchman feels he is man; perhaps that is what distinguishes him most from other men. It was a dream of many that they were now about to finish once and for all with the bloody and primitive custom, the atrocity of solving problems by force of arms. They were marching to the last of all wars.

You set out a colonel, commanding a brigade. In the very line of fire begins your experience of active warfare. You go out in person to order, inspire, and lead your group.

Here you ought to be blamed, sir, for needlessly having exposed the precious life of a leader, if this temerity, in a man as cool and self possessed as yourself, did not signify something quite other than an impulse of bravado or a longing for action. Danger or no, you were avid for the real thing, you whose skepticism is severe on theory. You needed close observation of man under fire. The unorthodox professor of tactics was not content with seizing on and exposing the naïve errors of the peacetime systems of strategy. Where the fire was falling he had to lay up his store of practical experience.

Above all, you felt it was of the first importance for a

leader himself to undergo the strong emotions of the soldier, to feel in his own flesh the upheavals, the reflex actions, the sudden fluctuations of energy, to see the real effects of orders upon the troops, and finally to realize that the possible is not the same, when viewed from headquarters, as when viewed by the squad.

You confirmed that your previous ideas were sound, that your uneasiness as to our accepted rules of warfare was too well-founded. A wide area of territory is yielded. Superior tactics allow the enemy strategy scope to develop its full-scale plans. Soon we are universally believed to be lost, and virtually we are. Our eastern bulwarks are largely outflanked. We cannot hold out in the north, or in Lorraine. At Guise, Lanrezac (once your colleague at the École de Guerre) strikes a telling blow in vain at the advancing troops; it cannot prevent the wide enemy wing from closing on our left and skirting Paris. The art of war is about to triumph. A strategy in the grand manner, imbued with contempt for the enemy, nearly faultless tactics, a crushing weight of arms, superlative troops—how could the assurance of approaching victory not rest secure on all this? Who has ever seen a beaten army, retiring in disorder, growing weaker perforce, breaking up further with every step backwards, confused and hustled by the victor, suddenly turn face; suddenly grow so firm, and then so resistant, so disturbing, so vicious, transformed as by a miracle to the point where the pursuer must stand, take the defensive, grow nervous, break line, and finally dig in to escape the worst; into the very earth, where they will stay for four years, until the defeat, until the calamitous ending of the almighty offensive that was to be completed in *thirty-three days*? What a collapse of splendid calculations!

For there had been born in the French, without their own or anyone else's knowledge, a valor altogether new, an incredible tenacity, unexampled in their annals, a marvelous solidarity. Through four endless years, this volatile, this capricious race will be seen, in spite of the heaviest losses, the most agonizing setbacks, not only to hold out, and to multiply the fiercest onslaughts, but even more, to inspire, rouse, strengthen their allies, whom they comfort, whom they arm, whom they train, while it remains inconceivable how they find such resources in themselves, so much spirit, and heart, and money, and heroes, expending more of all these in one war perhaps than they had ever done through the whole length of France's history.

Joffre, on the Marne, exemplifies this new firmness of the French. He demands, he secures, he embodies it.

It is remarkable how our people on this occasion met the strange nervousness of the enemy leaders with the extraordinary calm, deliberation, the simple and decisive judgment of our general. He knows that squalls will pass, that the thing is not to push but to endure; he draws back, he has the strength to await the day when chances are most in his favor. Then he gives the signal, throws down his cards, and wins.

The Marne campaign stretched on and terminated with the Yser, perhaps Foch's masterpiece. The strategic impetus of the Germans is smashed on that stream and expires at Ypres. There, after that furious race in which he overtakes the enemy, Foch draws together the English, the Belgians, persuades them to hold out in the ruins and sandhills, wins them over to his method of defense, which is to attack without ceasing; and finally fixes the field of action. A peculiarly important victory, and the last example of classical strategy in the West. Note that this deathblow was administered by Foch; it was reserved for the grand strategist to close the issue for strategy, exterminate it. From now on, no more hoping for a decision, an emergency, a lightning blow. Goodbye to the dreams of another Austerlitz or Sedan! . . . For now comes the reign of endurance, of impregnable defenses, and all the heresies come into force; from now on the only objectives are geographical, and now begins the evolution of the most complex equipment imaginable. It is no longer a case of convincing the enemy of his defeat, surrounding him, administering a sure deathblow; no longer any relying on the mobility of troops, but rather of acting on a closed front with the properties of a live equilibrium, bending, undulating—but re-forming, re-closing, and never failing to envelop, or limit, or paralyze any action to break it.

No longer can war be the accelerating, converging drama it used to be, and was still hoped to be. In future the enemy will have to be exhausted gradually, division after division, and onwards into the depths of the nation behind the lines, to the last man, the last penny, the last ounce of energy. War is no longer an action but a condition; a fearful sort of regime; it has taken up residence—but alas, on our own soil!

Not a moment, sir, not an incident of this new and terrible experience but prompts your reflections and teaches you some new principle. Whatever action you appear in, you are enlarged by it: in Artois, commanding a corps, in Champagne an army. But each of these trials convinces you more of the illusion of those who still believe that a penetration of fronts and a battle in open terrain will finish the war; an illusion which persists in haunting those minds conditioned only by history, more obsessed with striking precedents than prepared to study the present for what it rejects and what it demands.

But the problem, it must be admitted, was the same for both sides, and equally insoluble, the situations terribly frozen. While the means become more and more powerful, impotence itself only grows. Setbacks become the rule. In each camp offensives and defensives follow each other as if in rotation, a continual exchanging of roles. The war from December 1914 to July 1918 is summed up in bloody fumblings and gropings, confused trials of the old and the new, under conditions never dreamed of, fit to confound the ablest minds. Napoleon risen from the tomb could have made no better of such a plight.

In all, the sheer size of the armies, the total commitment of each nation, the fixed nature of the fronts, the use of weapons and defenses that forbade all movement, the resulting stalemate obliging the command more and more to worry about its rear, about politics, opinion, economic survival—all this reduced the directing minds of the opposed armies to the same alternations of impulse and objection, trial and renouncement.

That is why we need not search too deeply into the reasons for the grand offensive of Verdun. Those which the Germans have given are not totally convincing, or indeed consistent. The facts are simple. We need only put ourselves for a moment in the soldier's place. No one knows what to do, and yet something must be done—grand and irresistible reason. There is no obvious course, strategy is tied up in knots. Up till now every offensive has failed. Imagination, beggared, can only suggest what it has thought of before; only this time, the blow will be much harder. This attack will be mounted on a tremendous scale. Four hundred thousand soldiers; an incredible force of artillery concentrated on one point of the front; the Crown Prince as leader; for objective, a strong point famous in history—and there you have the battle of Verdun.

A battle? . . . Say Verdun was a war in itself, lodged within the Great War, rather than a battle in the accepted sense. Verdun was something else besides. Verdun was a duel before a world audience, a strange and almost symbolic wrestling match, where you were the champion of France, face to face with the Crown Prince. The world looks on. The fighting, which each side in turn initiates or resists, will last almost a year. I will not retrace its episodes or phases, nor retail the history of your part, which belongs to each and every moment of it. I will signalize only a few traits—some with reference to your mind, for it was now that your purely experimental concept of warfare is proven and triumphs, some regarding your character—and not forgetting your heart.

Sir, you at Verdun took on, organized, and assumed in your own person that immortal resistance which gradually, in your controlling grasp, as though by a subtle and astonishing change of key, was transformed into an offensive reaction, and then, to the amazement of the world and the confusion of the enemy, into a powerful pressure, a retaking of lost positions, into a victorious counterattack.

On the evening of 25 February 1916, the moment you were appointed you flew, through snow and darkness, to make contact with all the defense headquarters. At midnight you dictate a vital order, repudiating the purely instinctive tactics of local defensive fighting in isolation, foot to foot, for every inch of territory. You hand out to each unit its part in an overall plan. You know the enemy presses where we are worn down, and that the only way to hold out is to concentrate all resistance at a point strong enough in itself and strongly fortified. The assault is held. But the attacks are so powerful and persistent that exposed units melt away in a few days under the furious fire of thousands of weapons of every caliber. And this fire is trained so heavily on your lines of communication that the front is in danger of foundering from lack of munitions, food, supplies of all kinds.

Then it was that you created that truly Sacred Way, continually broken up by the wheels, the marching feet, rains, and mortar fire; but continually refilled with the very stones of the country by an army of workers; continually beaten in and trampled by the troops and convoys as they come and go between life and the firing line. You had demanded the perpetual replacement of the defending troops, and laid down the system whereby every corps in the Army took its turn at Verdun. Turn by turn they went. They came back muddy, broken, haggard—and venerable. They all came to Verdun, as though to undergo some inexpressible consecration, as though every province of the country had to take part in that supreme sacrifice of the war, above all others bloody and solemn—in the gaze of the whole world. It seemed as if they went up, by that Sacred Way, to some unexampled oblation, at the most fearful altar ever raised by man. Between French and Germans, it consumed five hundred thousand victims in a few months.

Let us talk no more of the heroes of antiquity, or even those of Napoleon! They had only to endure for a matter of hours; they had enemies they could see and approach; they had open air and movement; and no gas, no floods of flame, no entombment in the mud, no annihilation from the sky, no nights of dazzling terror; and in those days man had not learned how to cover a field of carnage with a fearful cloud-burst of millions of bullets and bursting shells.

Truly, modern man—the ordinary man, as a soldier, in spite of all that was said and thought of his loss of character his softening by a more artificial or refined existence, by pleasure, by lack of faith—during this war reached the highest point ever attained by man at any time, as regards energy, resignation, willing subjection to hardship, suffering, and death.

That was how Verdun was saved. From that great name yours is inseparable. But your suffering was immense. While you inspired in all a confidence no other chief could impart, while all relied on you, and your presence at once reassured army, government, the nation, the high command, and the allies, you, the all-too-lucid witness of the enemy's huge exertions, of the losses and the unimaginable trials of our troops, you, still always in doubt of keeping your last lines intact, until the very end you refused to cry victory. It even gave you a sort of uneasiness to know that opinion behind the lines was anticipating the event, baptizing as a victory what was still only an unbeaten resistance. That is altogether you. You have no patience with what is neither assured nor demonstrable. You are no friend to appearances.

But what feelings you had for those men whose unspeak-able hardships, whose fatigues and sufferings, whose mutilated bodies and corpses were the stuff of salvation!

Sir, your apparent coldness and severity is sufficiently deceiving. It fails to betray the admiration, the solicitude, the fatherly affection which you feel for your soldiers. But there was never a leader more aware of their needs, more careful of their strength, more opposed to excessive rigor or superfluous demands—and above all more anxious to spare their lives. Little by little the soldier learned to know you; he discovered in you the man who, however remote his rank, never made himself unapproachable, inaccessible, a being of another species.

Besides, your mind is too closely at grips with the reality of war, too convinced of the importance of its practical execution—by neglect of which even the finest plans are mere paper—not to keep the sense of the fighting soldier and his condition forever present, active in your designs. For what is it to command, if it be not to govern forces with the thinking mind and to temper that thinking with an exact assessment of those forces? As the mind, when it has a strong and clear sense of its body and limbs, feels more the master of itself and reality, so it is with high command. You could not bear to command in the abstract, without partaking of the mind and being of those who carried out your orders. This, sir, was what gave you, at the cruelest and most fearful conjuncture, the means—and the glory— of saving not only our forces, but the honor, and perhaps even the very existence of our country.

Verdun, tremendously assailed and tremendously held, had called only for the deployment of your splendid military abilities, in an action involving immensely elaborate application; but you had only a foreign enemy to deal with. Toward the end of the following spring looms the danger of dangers. Our army, engaged in a huge operation which was to be decisive, filled and almost intoxicated with the highest hopes, suddenly finds itself stalled in the middle of the struggle whose vast aim still seems impossibly out of reach.

73

It falls back from the height of its hopes, exhausted and having suffered serious losses—which rumor exaggerates. Above all, it is bitterly disillusioned. Inadequate preparations, rash acts which had not escaped the eye of such seasoned soldiers, unforgivable blunders, all these contributory causes of the setback, obvious to all, return to people's minds and add to the most widely varied motives for discontent: promises never kept, insufficient resting periods, excess of fatigues and pointless exercises.

Murmurs begin to rise (and not only on the part of the troops) against the high command. Alarming incidents break out here and there. Riddled with sinister rumors, exposed defenseless to every hint, our heroic Army is ready to waver. It begins to listen to disquieting voices, voices that spread among anxious multitudes just what is needed to lend point to their anger and direct their impulses. There are promptings to refusal of duties, even to open rebellion.

Will the extreme danger point be reached? Who will deliver us out of this pass? Who will put new life into these regiments that seem as though infected by a sudden break-up of their will to fight and conquer? All the hopes, the valor, the smashed endeavors are turned into a threatening, muddied ferment, into acts of violence and near-revolt. We must never forget that in France the most forceful revolutionary movements were always unleashed by patriotic anger.

Who will deliver us from this pass? Only one name is on people's lips. Only one man, at a time when we have encountered risks unheard-of, is capable of parrying this greatest risk of all.

The danger itself, common sense, and power all point to him. A minister is inspired to name him; and on the hour, as at Verdun, the mere news that you have been called upon is a relief to anguished minds. What an honor, sir, to receive at so terrible a conjuncture the burden of full control, to be the obvious choice of all as the one man whom circumstances proclaim to be the only alternative to destruction!

Your famous predecessor knew an equal glory, when the whole pressure of imminent disaster, in 1918, put him at the head of the four armies, in a matter of hours.

So you are made supreme head, master of our destinies, commander of the whole French Army. At once you emerge in all your wisdom, and presently, in all your humanity.

At this moment, before all else, alas, you have to live through the most painful hours of your life. You have to strike. "*But*," you write, "*these are our soldiers who, for three whole years, have been with us in the trenches!*"

One day History, with facts and figures in hand, will point out all the moderation in your severe measures. In a matter of weeks, without hatred and without fear, you repressed mutiny, punished weakness among the leaders and criminal acts among the troops; and in person you probe to the deepest causes of the ill. You make inquiries in this cantonment and that. You speak from man to man, bringing with you just rewards, equality in the turns of service, of trench duty and leave. Discerning the moral and material motives behind the bitterness and irritation, you take anxious care for the men's feeding, rest, and entertainment; and you reassure them too of our hope in arms—which you alone can do without being suspected of rhetoric or illusions. Above all, you decree that their lives should in no case be risked in fruitless or ill-prepared actions.

Finally the miracle at which all must bow is accomplished,

all the dissatisfied are converted, all our heroic rebels are won back to their Fatherland.

A victory without precedent in military annals, a singular renewal, for which the talents of a great commander would not have sufficed; it needed the spirit of a great and just man.

I cannot but emphasize at this point that it was the very general who was sometimes said to *look on the black side*, to forecast the worst, who was unanimously called upon to restore hope and inspire fresh ardor in our troops.

The Army once reassured was subjected by you, throughout its ranks, to fresh training—a few paces away from the enemy lines. Not the least strange feature of the war was the need to learn how to wage it while waging it. To instill every mind with your tactics was your prime endeavor, you want to be sure that all you have studied and learnt from the first entry into war should inform the smallest detail of the exercises carried out on the margin of combat.

In a few months, under your expert hands, the French Army develops into an incomparable instrument of force, precision, and toughness; through the years of crisis and decision it will prove, between the English Army, soon to be put to the fiercest trials, and the slowly growing, slowly preparing American Army, to be the essential agent of the common defense and victory.

What a spectacle, that final year of the war!...Everyone can feel the end approaching, but the end is still veiled. It is still possible to doubt the issue. The enormity of the consequences of defeat stiffens armed resistance on both sides. With Russia gone from the scene, Germany concentrates its forces. But if the moment favors her, time is working on our side. And everything commits them to the policy of solving the issue with one supremely violent thrust. Their attacks are masterly, winning fearful successes in a few hours. And these force the stricken allies into a move which wisdom would have dictated from the start.

It is now that Foch emerges from the twilight where he had lingered ever since the Somme. That great leader had never yet had the leader's command. And never, besides, was there a war less apt to his genius than this one of detail and suspense. He was born for actions of the noblest sweep, and he is only his true self in movement and maneuver on a grand scale. Action inhabits and commands his every thought. Here we have a Frenchman of epic mind.

What struck one first about him was the extraordinary quickness of his ideas, marked by the irresistible rush of his words—as though in a hurry to penetrate the thought of his interlocutors and get in one word ahead at the strategic goal in question. It was transparently impossible for him to endure holding back the spark which had just struck his mind. Instinctively he made for the heart of the matter; the moment it was formed his thought would fly to the decisive act, would at once envisage the fullest possible development of it; sacrificing detail, at times defying the possible.

He was very ready with images—the quickest if not always the safest means of transport between two flashes of inspiration. He was accused of obscurity, a reproach often leveled at the most lucid minds, which do not always find common expressions the best means of clarity. I remember, however, during one of the last sittings of the Academy at which he was present, while we were—very placidly— debating the idea of our French Grammar, Foch, asked in turn for his opinion, said: "Let it be short and simple." He liked only what went straight to the point. But different minds admit of very different trajectories in the way of *straight lines*. Every way of thinking has its own short cuts.

Foch was the very soul of energy. A man of this type is invariably, irresistibly drawn to the decision that demands the highest energy in its conception and execution; an inestimable quality in a calling whose sole aim is to procure or to avoid an irreversible result.

At times it might have been said that Foch, shrugging off the present, rejecting what everyone could see, brushing aside the real as an illusion, loved purely and simply to set his will against circumstances. He seemed convinced that all must bow to a determined will, strangely above the realities of the moment, locked in its own absolute aloofness, almost indifferent to any material inconsistency between forces and means; a man less affected by what he sees than by what he seeks.

It can happen that such driving forcefulness leads to rashness, and formidable reverses can sometimes break it. But a very simple reflection justifies it in all cases where the situation is most grave, which are the vital ones in war. For when all seems lost, when everything that transpires, every approaching sign is one of menace, or even complete despair, where can the last hope be lodged, the sole remaining chance be found, in a complex of conditions and events which shapes hour by hour toward disaster? This final chance and hope is and can only be in the very heart of the enemy. In the midst of the greatest gains, the soul of the near-victor still has its weaker side. The shadow of doubt that remains as to his approaching victory, or else his over-drunken confidence in it, these are the final opportunities of the side that feels its end near.

This was what was always in Foch's mind, and what saved us. In the days of deepest crisis he can sense despair behind the fury, and even behind the fearful advances made by the enemy. There he saw their weak spot. There he could see victory dawning so distinctly that even the dire succession of events, the battle that pushed to Amiens, the battle near Compiègne, the terrible surprise attack at Château-Thierry, hardly delayed the project of his grand offensive.

Now at last is the time when he can come into his own. The half-year, thronged with reverses, draws to a close. Summer begins. Foch takes victory in hand, leads it on all fronts. With autumn comes triumph.

What a moment that must have been for him, when the salvation of his country, his lifelong ambition, the crowning of all his mental efforts, the certainty of his own immortal fame were all in one offered to him by a few bewildered and stupefied men, with shame and rage in their faces, endless bitterness in their souls: and in their hands, all their country has left to give!

I will not venture, sir, to talk of these events after you, who lived, endured, or created them, in a continual and inspired collaboration with Marshal Foch. The far south, the far north of France blended their natures and their contrasting virtues for the service and safety of the nation, one and indivisible, and for the reuniting to the national body of those French people who had been cut off from it.

Alas, one has to admit that not all the aims of the war were realized.

The hope above all to see finally lift the constricting anxiety which had weighed on Europe for so many years has not been fulfilled. But perhaps we should never look to war—or even to political action—for the power to establish a genuine peace?

Thirteen years after, the sky is still far from clear; and the world, sir, is in no hurry to grant you the leisure which you have so splendidly deserved. France, to her great regret, is in no position to let you cultivate at ease your flowers and your vineyards, down there at the foot of the Alps and just above the sea. She means to cultivate her own lands in peace, at the cost of yours. You are still the inspiration and the discipline of her Army; you review her troops, retraining some, and putting fresh heart into others; you watch over her defenses; you have journeyed down the whole line of her frontier, in the company of the dearest disciple and warmest friend of Marshal Foch, and have studied with your own eyes every position on that sacred line.

Needs must. We are too wealthy in the eyes of some, too well-armed in the eyes of others; and for others, we have too much territory; and so we are a provocation to the world, not in our own words or aims, but simply because of what we are, and what we have.

But how can any sane mind still dream of war, still cling to any illusion about its effects, or look to war for what peace cannot obtain?

Let us talk only reason. In former times a war, after all, could be justified by its results. It could be considered, if only with a ruthless eye, as a passage by way of arms from one definite position to another. It could be calculated. It was a business between two sides, settled by two armies. The quarrel was confined; the pieces in the game were numbered; and then the victor took his spoils, grew richer, greater, and enjoyed a prolonged advantage from his gains.

But the world of politics has changed indeed; and the

cold common sense which in the past could speculate on the profits of a bloody enterprise has to admit today that its forecasts may be hopelessly wide of the mark. For now there can be no longer any localized conflict, limited duels, closed systems of warfare. He who goes to war can no longer guess against whom or with whom he will finish it. He is involved in an incalculable risk, against undetermined forces, for an indefinite length of time. And even if the issue is favorable, at the very moment of victory, he will have to dispute the fruits of it with the rest of the world, and perhaps give in to the rulings of those who took no part in the contest. All he can be sure of is the immense losses in human life and goods which he must suffer without compensation; for in an age whose tremendous powers of production can be turned to destruction in a few days, in a century when every discovery, every invention, is as much a menace as a boon to the human race, the losses will be such that, whatever demands may be made of the vanquished, they will be only a miserable fraction of the immense resources consumed. These are certainties. To them may be added another formidable factor; I mean the strong likelihood of internal disorders and upheavals of incalculable scope.

What I have said, I believe, only applies to what we have already seen: two opposed groups of nations devouring each other to the point of final exhaustion on the part of the chief adversaries; every economic and military forecast proved wrong; peoples who believed themselves remote in intention and situation from any involvement forced to join in the combat; ancient and powerful dynasties dethroned; Europe's primacy in the world compromised, her prestige whittled away; the value of the mind, and things of the mind, gravely threatened; daily life disrupted and made much harder; anxiety and bitterness almost everywhere; violent or minority regimes taking control in various countries.

Let no one believe that a fresh war could improve matters, or make the human lot more pleasant once more.

Yet it seems as though experience were not enough. Some place their hopes in a renewal of the slaughter. They feel there was not enough of distress and disillusion; not enough ruins and grief; not enough of the maimed, the blind, the widowed, and the orphaned. It seems as though the problems of peace have dimmed the atrocities of the war—whose fearful images are even banned in some quarters.

But is there a single nation among those who desperately fought who would not gladly wish the gigantic struggle had been only a horrible nightmare, from which they could have awakened, shuddering but unharmed, terrified but sober? Is there a single nation among those capable of daring the bloody enterprise that can firmly look its intention in the face, weigh the unknown chances, envisage, not simply the ever-present possibility of defeat, but all the actual consequences of a victory—if we can really talk of victory in an age when war, raised to the power of natural cataclysms, can carry out the indiscriminate destruction of all life, on each side the frontier, throughout the most heavily populated territories?

How strange an epoch! Or rather, how strange the minds that can be responsible for such thoughts! In full awareness, fully conscious of their aims, in the face of terrible memories, and innumerable graves, the ordeal scarcely over—while the mysteries of cancer and tuberculosis are being passionately probed in the laboratories—there are men who can still dream of playing the game of death.

Just a hundred years ago, Balzac wrote: "Without even taking the time to wipe her feet steeped in blood to the ankles, has not Europe always been prepared to go to war afresh?"

Might we not be tempted to say that humankind—however lucid and rational it be—incapable of sacrificing its urges to its knowledge, and its hatreds to its sorrows, behaves like a swarm of absurd and pitiable insects, irresistibly drawn by the flame?

Commencement Address to the Legion of Honor's School for Girls at Saint-Denis

Young ladies,

WHEN our Chancellor paid me the honor of asking me to preside at this ceremony, I, as a member of the Legion, could only bow before the authority of his high office. Still, the prospect troubled me deeply. I began to feel as timid as a young girl.

I know of course that girls are by no means so timid as people say, or perhaps as people would sometimes like. I have noticed that what little timidity remains in the world is scarcely to be met with except among members of the Institute, particularly when they have to appear in uniform. Believe me, among my colleagues I have seen famous writers and even Marshals of the Army who had commanded millions of men completely intimidated by the idea that they were going to speak before an audience composed almost entirely of ladies.

My task here seems to me even more difficult and frightening, for young ladies are far more to be feared than grown ones. Being more spontaneous, they poke fun more readily. That is why the very idea of having to address you on a solemn occasion and in this majestic outfit has transformed me (inwardly, I mean) into a bashful girl.

This young person could not even dream of offering you advice based on vast experience, as my friend Judge Lescouvé did three years ago; even less, give you lessons of heroism as did the illustrious and much regretted General Archinard.

The truth is really this: the flattering assignment to give you a little sermon seemed to me the most delicate and demanding task that my election to the Academy has yet brought me.

It was no use my striving to raise my spirits by trying to picture the mysterious enclosure of your buildings, entirely unknown to me, established and as it were consecrated by the Emperor himself in the shadow of the royal and mortuary Basilica. I found no hint of how to speak to you within these venerable walls where so many young ladies have (I hope) learned so many things, where so much of the future takes shape, where, from day to day and from year to year, under the solicitous eye of those who instruct you, you gradually become yourselves.

I asked myself: what shall I say to them? They are more learned than I am, for they are going to school and studying for examinations—and those are the only opportunities given us mortals to know something, for a few days. . . .

And so, hesitant and miserable, I racked my mind in vain for something good, useful, and seemly to entertain you.

It was no use recalling that Racine had written two masterpieces for young ladies, and that those two *divertissements* given at Saint-Cyr are still admired by everyone who knows how to read—to read in a way that has been almost forgotten in our day. To read. . . .

Reading, I said to myself. There's a glimmer of hope. There's something that is rather in my line, and important enough for me to talk about to this terrifying young audience of Saint-Denis. I shall tell them . . . And now here I am telling you: Young ladies, you who are the peculiarly French

85

children of France, I have no doubt that among the many subjects offered you, you have a special interest in the literature of our country, the most literary country in the world, and the last, perhaps, where the concern with form persists, even though already sadly diminished.

I do not doubt that most of you, even those who dissect frogs or tease out second degree trinomials, have a certain taste for our great writers. I'll even wager that some of you keep hidden away—more or less—in a corner of your desks a mysterious notebook full of your own productions, the trial flights of fledging talents, in verse or prose.

Indeed, nothing is quite so charming as the first gleams of poetic talent, the self coming awake amid the beauties and resources of its native tongue. One day the magic spell of the word falls over us, and the Universe of Speech appears.

Words take shape, and *things* sing forth their *names*. The dreariest dictionary comes to life as a forest of suggestions, as a confused presence of all possible works, of all the fine lines not yet composed, of all the intellectual or musical resonances as yet unheard. Even dusty old *Grammar* and its crazy companion, *Syntax*, suddenly begin to have a fascination of their own—and all those tricky *Parts of Speech*, watched over by ferocious *Participles*, followed in order of precedence by an army of *Clauses*—principal, subordinate, object, circumstantial, and all the rest of the capricious crew. Meanwhile, trailing far behind the endless procession parading hosts of examples, a grumbling and wretched old man, shunned by all, drags himself along, that fallen nobleman: the *Imperfect Subjunctive*. Now of course, my young friends, it is not the coils of vocabulary and syntax that first attract us to literature. Just remember how the Word first enters our life. Even before people have stopped singing us the songs

86

that make the newborn babe smile and sleep, the age of stories begins. The child drinks them in like its mother's milk. He demands that these marvels continue and be repeated. He makes a pitiless and excellent audience. No one would guess how many hours I have spent dreaming up magicians, monsters, pirates, and fairies to satisfy children who keep saying, "Go on, go on," to their exhausted father.

But finally the day comes when they can read, and nothing could be more crucial. It is the third capital event in our life. The first is learning to *see*; the second, learning to *walk*; and this is the third, *reading*, by which we enter into possession of universal knowledge. Before long we are slaves to reading, chained by the ease with which it allows us to enter into extraordinary lives, to experience powerful sensations through the mind alone, to live through prodigious adventures that leave us where we started, to act without acting, to have, almost without effort, thoughts more striking and profound than our own—in other words, to add to what we are and might be an infinite member of feelings and imaginary experiences and observations that are not ours.

They say the same thing happens when we sleep. We can live a whole life in a few seconds by the clock. So, through reading we may live out an entire existence in an hour, or the mysterious operation of a poem may transform a few otherwise insignificant instants into a miraculously ordered and decorated interval of time, a jewel for the soul. The poem may even become a kind of magic formula, a talisman that our heart can recall in moments of strong emotion or enchantment when we fail to find a sufficiently pure or forceful expression of what moves us.

I know of a man who underwent a painful operation in

which no anesthetic could be employed. He found a kind of relief, and easing of the pain and a renewal of his strength and patience, by reciting one of his favorite poems to himself during the lulls between the worst moments.

Such is the power of art. You know it as well as I, but we have not finished with one another. I have only now reached the point where I have something to say.

This ease with which, while reading—that is, while submitting to the action of literature—we leave behind what surrounds us, and even what we are, in order to follow the thread of a story, or to enter into the suppleness, the grace, the solemnity, and the rhythmic power of poetry, is remarkable. It is worth our thinking about it a little.

As the snake obeys the snake-charmer's flute, as the wolves in the legend followed the fiddler's violin, and as the beasts obeyed Orpheus, thus the mind follows the play of words and develops a kind of secret power within itself. Storytellers, poets, even philosophers know particularly well how to play on this verbal faculty in order to amuse or move or develop other minds.

The truth is that literature is only a kind of speculation, a development of certain properties of language, in particular those which happen to be the most lively and effective among primitive peoples. The more beautiful the form, the closer it is to the origins of consciousness and expression: the more skillfully it is employed, the more it strives to rediscover through a kind of synthesis the fullness and wholeness of the spoken word still fresh and growing. Rhythm, balanced sonorities of timbres and accents, abundance of imagery, the energy and aptness of strokes, turns, and flourishes of speech—those characteristics are scarcely to be found or looked for any longer except in poetry. Sophisticated ancients like us speak a highly abstract language, over-complicated by its burden of meanings, over-simplified by what it sacrifices in using formulas, abbreviations, and the brutal economy of telegraphic style. Both inhuman and vulgar, slack and overloaded, our language is shot through with technical, political, and administrative jargon, full of clichés and monstrous formations, perfectly fitted for transacting business and relaying signals in this mechanized world, like the old signal towers along a railroad line, and perfectly useless as a means of bringing into play the deepest and noblest portions of our beings.

All that, my dear young ladies, all the simplifications and makeshifts the modern age demands, all the conveniences it offers in expediting relations between men, the haste it forces on us or at least suggests, the abuse of the marvelous means of acting and feeling created by science and multiplied by industry, means which tend to spare us any exertion, and to substitute images for the imagination, impressions for careful reflection, the instant for any space of time—all these precious creations threaten the very qualities from which they arose.

What creations? What qualities?

What are we losing, or at least what do we run the risk of losing because we have acquired such domination over nature?

At what price have we gained these victories? We have conquered space, shrunk time, overcome darkness, the sea around us, the air above us. We have harnessed matter and the energy it holds. We are even beginning to enter spheres of action whose extent we cannot fully imagine. Everything that happens on the entire globe can be transmitted instantaneously into the same room with us. We can hear anything that makes a sound. Everything that has taken place can be preserved in material inscriptions or impressions, and thus we sometimes have the miraculous and poignant experience of seeing people now dead in the act of laughing and of hearing them talk.

Miracles they are indeed—yet miracles that come along so fast that we can scarcely react to fresh news of further marvels. Children take airplanes as much for granted as we took the horse and carriage; they turn the dial on a radio as easily as we turned the pages of a picture book, and they listen to the universe the way we listened to the talk of people going by our windows, and to the hurdy-gurdy and all the old-world noises of a city street.

But man does not live by surprises and miracles alone. Moreover he is and always will be the *supreme miracle* in his own eyes, the essential wonder; and every new prestige he creates for himself—without knowing how or why he does so—leaves him still an enigma to himself. When he grasps this thought, the man of today surrounded by his inventions feels like a grown-up child in the midst of the extraordinary toys and games he has built for himself. Terrifying toys some of them are. He is amazed that he ever put so much talent and energy into discovering how to send from one end of the world to the other, with the speed of light, a popular song, a picture postcard, a bouquet of flowers, or a ton of explosive.

We must admit that the mood of the age is divided between anxiety and a sense of futility. Try to guard against those two enemies of the human race. You are getting ready for life; here, on the benches of this school, you are preparing for the substance of your later thoughts. You are forming the future, constructing, without knowing it, the framework for your ideas to come. The women you are to become will think, reason, decide, and express opinions according to the patterns and the language you are busy acquiring here in your student years at Saint-Denis.

Well then, my dear young ladies, these patterns and this language are here communicated to you in the most appreciative fashion, for your teachers ask you to observe closely and breathe deeply of the very flower of literature, the time-honored works of our most perfect writers. You are learning to appreciate what is most elegant, profound, and solid in the vast treasure of our literature. Let it be your favorite food. Do not learn to look at it as a wretched business for study courses, a bitter medicine for examinations. Read closely and weigh every word. You will feel the breathing life of the mind itself, and afterwards it will be as though you had thought and created yourselves. I believe everyone in himself amounts to no more than what he can say to himself, which means what he knows how to say. Learn to do this with the respect, precision, sincerity and grace worthy of a precious young life. By doing so, you will have learned how to write.

Let me add that conditions appear perfect at Saint-Denis for this training of the mind.

I visited your grounds yesterday; I had never suspected they were so vast, so rich in historic beauty, and so well adapted to their modern use. This is a perfect environment for work, and I know more than one writer who would be happy to settle in it.

Your Headmistress guided my steps, which were far more numerous than I would have expected. She smiled at my wonderment. Confidentially, kind as she was, I think she enjoyed startling the Academician and leaving him breathless, while receiving him with a perfect hospitality that touches him deeply.

I had the impression of being in a place composed from all that was noblest in our history.

At the gate of this building the bustle and self-defeating confusion of modern life die away. In this famous abbey, constructed long ago by men who were of one mind about creating the imposing intimacy necessary for meditation and the kind of work whose aim is to endure, you find the now priceless luxury of silence, a magnificently well proportioned space, and the majesty of the great ages. Through these huge windows your youthful eyes look out on the flower beds and long vistas of an immense park and, on the other side, on the steeples and pinnacles and the great rose window and the stained glass of one of the finest buildings of the Middle Ages. You can feel wonderfully isolated from an era that knows how to achieve enormous size in its buildings, but no greatness; works that can be stunning, but not imposing; rigorous, but not pure. You are growing up in the shadow of France's most original and beautiful creations: her gothic and her classical styles.

Let me confess that if the little speech I had to prepare for you troubled me for a time, the visit to Saint-Denis has charmed me. Indeed, it has filled me with pride.

I travel quite often abroad, and often I cannot help being saddened by what I see there and fail to see here. I am shown universities, schools, and museums which do not make me very proud of some of ours. I think of everything France has accomplished, of everything she could accomplish, and I wonder about the future. Think about it sometimes, my dear young ladies, you who live in this building the like of which cannot be found abroad, think about the great works of France. You are her flesh and blood, you are a little of her future. All you have to do is to raise your eyes from your books to see the great monuments of the nation. You live and play and work in her very lap. Be proud of her for the rest of your lives.

On Henri Bremond

Gentlemen,

THE French Academy has been unable until now to pay Henri Bremond the public tribute it owes him, for he died far from Paris in a region of the Pyrenees he loved, and was buried in the noble Provençal city of his birth.

But it was the reverent thought of his faithful companion, whose lodgings adjoined his own, that the ancient house in which our admirable colleague had lived many years of his ardently studious life—between the venerable bulk of the cathedral and the literary monument he was building with scrupulous devotion—should bear a commemorative inscription, something simple, as befitting one who had given himself exclusively and passionately to the life of the mind.

Once this had been accomplished—this house now marked and dedicated to memory and to recognition—it was incumbent upon our Society to appear here, seconding the wishes of those who admired, loved, and sorely miss our great historian of Letters and the Inner Life.

It happens that I, the first to pay homage to Henri Bremond today, was bound to him by ties of friendship. This residence on the Rue Chanoinesse is a familiar sight to me. When Bremond chose his dwelling in this nook of the ancient island City of Paris, I often paid him a visit, to talk and sometimes to engage him in heated debate. Now I have returned to honor the memory of a dead man, but one more alive for me in death than many a living soul. . . . I can hear him, and see him.

I would climb the stairs and find him up there, his arms outstretched; he would rush to me, through the rather bare rooms, his mind fired by an idea or a beautiful line of poetry he had just discovered; or flaming with saintly wrath, he would lash out at the baseness of someone's soul, or the dullness of some book, or someone's stupidity or base stratagems.

Never was there a scholar more ebullient, an exegete more enthusiastic, a critic more intuitive or, for that matter, redoubtable than he—combining as he did the delicacy and fastidiousness of an extremely sensitive mind with his immense learning. He could bring to bear on the examination of a text or on the deciphering of an intention the kind of insight, the penetration that comes from the practice of hearing confession and inquiring into the depths of the soul, his own as well as others'.

Whenever I think of him, I see him moving about, growing excited, exclaiming, walking back and forth before that casement window which the cathedral fills with its mighty presence: Notre Dame, black and white, solid and pierced by light, chiming or mute—Notre Dame, historical, mystical, romantic, laden with meaning, with ornament and solemn memories.

This, Bremond's home, was indeed a Paris unto itself, some few steps away from the Paris that is constantly in flux.

It would take me only a few moments to overcome my astonishment that here it was still possible to side with Fénelon against Bossuet; that a mind could still be troubled, sincerely, by controversies which, though eternal, can scarcely be said to rage any longer, that someone could still feel, and feel to the point of violence, unwavering sympathy or antipathy for people and doctrines that have passed out of mind or are, today, mere names.

The books natural to this habitat outside our century came in large part from an age taken up with theology, the kind of books bought by the people of our world not to be read but to be used as ornaments for tables and walls, as candy-boxes, perfume-cases. . . . But here these folios and quartos from the splendid past, these noble books clothed in dark leather and yellowed vellum, had made fast friends with books of a very different sort. Our books, light in weight and of ephemeral substance, leaned against or were familiarly piled on top of these solid stacks of antiquated volumes. Bremond did not loathe all modern literature. Rather, he was one of those rare minds, in a highly unstable age given to sudden breaks with the past, who could discern and, better still, experience the continuity of literary ages and the survival of genuine values through the mutations of fashion and the surprises of novelty. Thanks to this great talent, we possess the many beautiful things he extracted from weighty tomes and the small print of pages in which they lay buried. He sensed what would please us, what would edify us in the wordy bulk of otherwise tedious treatises, in the murk of unreadable theologians. . . .

But the force and wealth of his mind were not confined to this. No one can forget, I least of all, to what singular lengths he carried his passion for poetry. In the life of this priest Bremond, poetry occupied a truly remarkable place. I do not know if he ever wrote verse, but I should be surprised if he had not tried his hand at it. I firmly believe that certain kinds of opinion concerning an art form cannot be preached without some practice. But practice itself will invariably lead the mind, provided it is not a mediocre one, to infinite reflection.

Thus Bremond meditated deeply on the art of the poet. He wrote brilliantly about it and we discussed the subject at great length. We rather liked to contradict one another, with an affection that made sport of our differences and derived strength from our opposite views. Poetry was the bond between us, a bond that if anything benefited from our occasional discords, as a lovely piece of music benefits from dissonant notes which bring it alive and make harmony, when it does return, the more appreciated.

I can only touch here upon the casuistry peculiar to these moot points of poetry, which cause dissension among those who enjoy discussing them even before they have so much as agreed on the meaning of the terms they use. I have only to recall the curious excesses of interpretation to which a great many excellent minds were led by two words I unfortunately wrote down one day: *pure poetry*. By these words, I meant to designate something very simple, a tendency toward the limits of an art, limits impossible to reach by means of language but none the less essential, as an idea and aspiration, to any poetic enterprise.

Yet the word *pure* is so beautiful that it transports the soul beyond finite meanings. Linked thus with the mysterious name *poetry*, it has the effect, through a kind of resonance, of dazzling the intellect and awakening, miraculously, all the higher powers in one's being—a thirst for some promise implicit in the sublimity we sense within ourselves.

The very expression is, then, an essentially *poetic* one, a complete poem two words long which inevitably had an

enormous effect on Bremond's mind and took on a tran-
scendent value of promise and beauty. He lavished heart and
mind on it, in dissertations you are familiar with. Inter-
rupting for a time the long labors required by his major opus,
he wrote several important essays on the theme of *pure
poetry.* I am convinced that he would not have minded if an
endless quarrel had ignited over this limitless subject, one
that would go on forever with replies followed by riposts
and counter-riposts, like those that once divided Court and
City, and Church doctors as well, in an age when questions
of grace, of frequent communion, or of essential baptism
were potentially explosive.

What made Bremond so unusual was that poetry and its
particular problems shared his mind with enthusiasms and
curiosities not ordinarily associated with a love for literature.
Those ancient sciences—theology and mysticism—together
with certain psychological investigations of a very modern,
subtle nature, seconded yet tempered his poetic craving for
the charming and the flawless. This combination of gifts
and far-ranging knowledge is rarely encountered, whether
in the larger world or in the fellowship of writers, among
whom he soon gained the reputation of being a wonderfully
complex and original personality.

He was a priest, and had been a Jesuit—a priest whose
faith never wavered, but whose mind revolved freely around
this fixed point. He was Provençal in origin, solidly nour-
ished on the literature of antiquity, a classicist by upbringing
and taste but romantic by instinct and inclination. Then too,
this man from Provence had lived many years in England,
whose language and poets he knew intimately; while there,
he associated not only with poets but with certain highly
abstract writers who, treading at times the indistinct frontier

between apologetics and psychology, at other times the borderline between Anglicanism and Roman Catholicism, absorbed themselves or consumed themselves in their desire to mend, by imperceptible degrees, what in their view should never have been sundered; they aspired, if you will, to find by the deepest observation of the soul the sources and impulses of belief.

Rarely has a single mind been able to follow so many lines of thought. He read (and as few can read) Mistral as well as Sophocles, Virgil as well as Shelley, Fénelon as well as Newman; he meditated on the *Grammar of Assent* yet derived the subtlest pleasure from Malherbe and Racine; over a long period he absorbed the lessons and discipline of his Order without surrendering a shred of his personality; and off and on, he participated in our literary life, observing our confusion, engaging in our debates as a partisan yet viewing them in the perspective of history; but then he would withdraw, take refuge effortlessly in his innermost self, regaining in some remote landscape the solitude where ideas gather and fall into place. All of this was brought harmoniously together in the astonishing conception of his major work, which his death interrupted.

I wonder if anyone realizes what is required of the mind that sets out to write a *History of Religious Feeling in France*. The thought of constructing a history of the most curious and most difficult to describe of all human feelings is in itself highly original. Whatever frame one chooses for it, even confining it to three centuries and limiting it to France, it is none the less an enterprise in the grand manner. To undertake it was a heroic decision; writing it exacted a labor and constancy unparalleled in our time.

It is in this work that our admirable colleague's varied

talents, his intellectual experiments, his far-reaching erudition, his artistic taste, his poetic sense, as well as his knowledge of theology and his studies of liturgy could be fused into an authoritative and well-constructed whole; and all of this was needed to create such a work. This unfinished history is, in the last analysis, an entirely original creation despite its erudite and critical trappings. And despite its imposing size, it moves along from volume to volume, fulfilling its intention, with a style and step so personal, so brisk, that the singularity of his treatise, the austerity of the subjects he is considering, the oblivion and disdain surrounding them today, the scientific apparatus of footnotes and references do not for a moment obscure the passionate presence of an author who is transcribing his very life. . . .

I cannot, here and now, gentlemen, elaborate on all the virtues of this prodigious work, on the extremely important analyses of prayer it contains, nor on its signal merit in having brought to light, to the greater glory of French letters, many admirable writers: masters of abstract style, of the expression of the soul's innermost workings, who at their best compare with our most illustrious authors. I am confident that all of these eminent qualities will be given appropriately full and specific acknowledgment when the Academy pays its solemn homage to the memory of Henri Bremond.

What I have said here is but a prelude in which I could not help confusing sentiment with duty and speak both as Director of the Company and as a friend who often used to come here, 16 Rue Chanoinesse, for a delightfully spirited hour.

This house on which Canon Dimnet, moved by feelings of friendly reverence, arranged to have Bremond's name inscribed, should not make us forget another of our colleague's residences—the one in which I first came to know him—the house on the Rue Méchain, in that singular quarter of Paris where Heaven and Hell, the Observatory and the Prison, convents and hospitals, meditation and madness, the astral telescope and the guillotine stand side by side. . . .

There, over a period of seven years, Henri Bremond resided, in the ever genial, affectionate company of the charming and venerable canon, Arthur Mugnier, one of those rare men who are *spirituel* in every sense of that ambiguous word and who, through their subtlety, their goodness, their devotion to the cult of souls and of letters, embody the ancient Church of France at its most exquisite. It was to the Rue Méchain that Maurice Barrès would diligently come for conversation with Bremond; it was there that Bremond learned from a sister of St Joseph of Cluny, who knew the uses of the telephone, the news of his election to the Academy; and it was there, a few moments later, that the Countess de Noailles appeared, bearing him a bouquet of flowers.

Gentlemen, she would be here . . .

Report on the Montyon Awards for Virtue

Gentlemen,

I MUST admit to being so innocent of the subject I am to discuss before you today that I cannot resist quoting a once-celebrated witticism and applying it to the present context.

Monsieur de Talleyrand, our famous compeer in the moral sciences, on being asked whether he believed in the Bible, answered that he had two invincible reasons for so doing: "In the first place," he said, "because I am Bishop of Autun; and, in the second, because I cannot make head nor tail of it."

I do not mean to imply by this that I understand nothing about virtue. I know perfectly well what it is not—and besides, I should not dare, at least not in public, confess an absolute ignorance of what it is; but, ultimately, I feel that the only virtue authorizing me to address myself to this great and venerable subject is my membership in your Society.

Thus, I had to spend a certain time wondering what I could possibly say to you and, conducting my thoughts as best I could in accordance with Descartes's precepts, I was led inexorably backward, in a series of logical inductions, to the first cause of the duty I am now striving to perform. At length my mind lighted upon the figure, or the Shade, of the man who arranged to have himself praised here in this hall on a certain day every year, a man who contrived to gain immortality by grafting his name, so to speak, on our own.

What a character was this magnificent Montyon! What depths of genius we must recognize in him, gentlemen!

Our institution was founded by a very great man. Richelieu seemed to sense, at the dawn of a resounding literary age, that the Republic of Letters must at last be founded, and he accordingly transformed a group of writers into an arm of the State by bringing our Academy into existence by decree and entrusting it with the care of our language and literature, which he considered, quite rightly, to be matters of national concern. But our illustrious founder was not sufficiently farsighted to see that one day his clear design would be obscured by a certain Montyon. Today we can afford to admire the feat of a mere private citizen who, two hundred years after the founding of the Academy, proved capable of altering its function radically by an act that cost him no more than a few written words—a bequest of money which we must award every year to Virtue.

Quite a remarkable investment, gentlemen. While we must agree that the names of our colleagues who are gone can scarcely be said to abide in everyone's memory, the name of Montyon will ring out beneath this dome once every year until the end of time.

Here was a maneuver so brilliant that we have reason to meditate on its author. It would be easy to lose oneself in conjecture over the motives of anyone wanting to do post-humous good. Would the idea of coming to the aid of Virtue ever occur to an essentially virtuous citizen? And the fact of insuring himself against oblivion by an endless bequest: must this not raise a certain doubt or even malicious conjecture concerning the motives of the giver?

103

La Rochefoucald, Stendhal, Forain, anyone with an eye for the worst, a pitiless student of the most likely motives that lie behind our acts, would doubtless seize upon this latent question and submit it to the whetted knife of his intelligence. He would want to know whether the funds did not come from some shady source, whether this gift and its stipulated purpose were not conscience money for ill-gotten gains or for a highly diversified secret life. Or perhaps—for no mind is quicker to imagine weakness in others than the mind that prides itself on intuition—our observer of the human heart would ascribe to Montyon the vanity of wishing to use Richelieu's work for his own glory, and of changing a society of minds into a charitable foundation by making us the accountants of his posthumous largesse.

But though it may be that for some men (even the great), evil is more plausible than good, and though their minds may be tempted or compelled to depreciate what they claim to understand, we shall not echo their abuses. Man is not so simple that it is sufficient to degrade him in order to know him. Let us therefore explore another hypothesis and assume that our generous Montyon had in mind a somewhat more elegant purpose.

It occurred to me, in the first place, that his idea of Virtue might not be the same as ours. Possibly this man, who brought about an essential reform in the Academy, observed that the latter had, insensibly and almost without thinking, allowed its initial literary ardor to cool, that the attention it had given during the first century of its existence to new creations of the human mind had wandered, that it sponsored ever fewer essay and poetry readings, that, lastly, the dictionary—which is our foremost endeavor—was advancing toward the Z of its day at a regally slow pace, not because our eminent colleagues were giving their painstaking attention to it but, rather, because their early ardor had grown sluggish. Voltaire, in his reception address, dared suggest "that there is reason to fear these honorable labors may slacken some day."

Monsieur de Montyon, judging us by appearances, as even today the public is often prone to do, may have thought that the Academy cared for next to nothing but its own glory, that it had to be provided with some entirely new function more noble than any it had hitherto performed, and so he assigned us the formidable task of giving Good its due, which cannot be done now without perpetuating his name. Ever since then, we have been a society half literary and half benevolent: the poet welcomed into our group must, when his turn comes, play moralist for a day.

It would seem, however, that on the whole we acquit ourselves rather well of our charitable assignment, that people willingly rely on our integrity, on our sense of justice, and above all, gentlemen, on our independence of mind for, since Montyon set the fashion, many people have placed their entire trust in us and followed his example in making us executors of their munificent intentions. Indeed, there are some evil minds who find us more able in matters of devotion, abnegation, or heroism than in our original role as state counsellors of the Republic of Letters. Yet even they sometimes show more leniency and often relent after paying us forty visits or so.

No, gentlemen, however much we are maligned, neither the quest for Good, nor its rewards, nor our discriminating comparisons of merit can compromise us in our foremost duty, such as we conceive and perform it. We remain above all guardians of the civil status of the French language, and I have an observation to make which, surprisingly, touches very closely on both the exercise of this office and the subject at hand, virtue.

VIRTUE, gentlemen, is a dead or at least a dying word. *Virtue* is rarely uttered nowadays. To the modern mind it does not present itself as the spontaneous expression of some reality impinging on our inner lives. No longer is it one of those particles of our living vocabulary that fall so freely and frequently from our tongues as to illustrate the real demands of our sensibility and our intellect. It is unlikely that any call for this word will issue from our depths; the chances are that one could live and reflect, act and meditate throughout the year without once feeling compelled to utter it, or even think it.

As for myself, I admit—and run the risks of such an admission—that I have never heard it, or (which is far graver), never heard it used but remarkably rarely in society, and always with ironic intent, which may indicate that I only frequent a rather wicked world, but I hasten to observe that I do not recall coming across it in the most widely-read, or for that matter the most highly-regarded, works of our time. Lastly, I know of no newspaper that prints it or, I fear, would dare print it except in some playful context.

It is, to be sure, a word still current in religious instruction where, within their special frame of reference, believers respond to it. Then, too, it has some currency in the Academy. . . . But even we, gentlemen, I dare say do little but associate it almost exclusively with the present occasion, with the prizes we announce, the accompanying speeches we deliver—so exclusively that, were it not for the benevolent

Montyon, this word, this poor word, would be nearing its end. *It has, to all intents and purposes, been abolished*, so to speak.

When *virtue*, a feminine noun, comes before us as she will before long to claim her due in some latter volume of the Dictionary, will we dare tell the truth, gentlemen? Will we have the courage to reveal this cheerless state of affairs? Will we declare that the word is so rarely used as to have become archaic? I am certain that we will not dare, that we would be ashamed to acknowledge the facts.

These facts cannot be gainsaid. Review your own experience. Consult your memories. Look about you and record what you see. Ask yourselves if the word *virtue* would spring to your lips or from your pen if it were not demanded by the occasion and, to be entirely honest, without causing you to feel vaguely insincere and out of joint with your time.

Our time lies within us, gentlemen, whatever we prefer to think; it is ourselves. If we discover *Virtue* languishing and disappearing from the common usage of this age, an age that is ours and ourselves, ought we not recognize our image in this discovery, question the death taking place within us, and grant that it may have some deeper meaning?

But before reflecting more closely on the matter, I shall not miss this precious opportunity to remind our Assembly to what extent its State-given authority—the function it performs of welcoming or eliminating elements of the language—can make the observer aware of many phenomena of social life which unfold so slowly as to be imperceptible at any given moment in time. A word that appears and takes root often embodies a world of relationships, it implies a complete sphere of activity; a word that loses something of its vigor or of its dominion, or of its recurrence, or of its spontaneity, a word honored only by us in our rather cautious dictionary, out of dutiful piety, for form's sake, like the ashes of a defunct idea—such a word, through its very decline, can still teach us something: death confers a kind of supreme meaning on the dying term.

What, then, are we to make of *virtue*'s passing, for such is the undeniable bent of the living language, such is the wretched condition to which I find the word reduced, once the most powerful and beautiful of words—one which rang out in Corneille and in the works of those who, like him, write in the grand style, one which enjoyed almost exorbitant, even startling favor in the following century when "men of feeling" used it so prodigally that we find it even in the Infernal Regions—of libraries, I mean.

What was its subsequent fate? Who became its chief spokesmen? As you know, gentlemen, the Revolution, when it came, adopted the word as its own, proclaimed it and grew drunk on it. That age was the true dictatorship of abstractions, and a virgin faith held all minds under the spell of their lucid delirium. Never have pure ideas been transformed so immediately and hysterically into acts. Never has a government spent such energy propounding the *Absolute* or imposing it on the governed. The time had seemingly come for Reason to assume command and for the Law to speak with indisputable power and authority. But reason is insignificant so long as it remains ideal; it will soon be betrayed if men are not inclined by nature to support it. Thus *Virtue* must reign officially alongside Reason, and advise the latter on the plans and acts of men in public office. So it came about that *virtue* made its debut in politics. Robespierre in particular cherished it, with a terrible conviction. On the tribune of the Convention, when the word

"Virtue" would ring out from the fatal perorations of the Incorruptible, it could be said of that extraordinary man, as it is said in Revelation, that "out of his mouth went a sharp two-edged sword."

But this, too, you know, gentlemen—we know all too well and through repeated experience—that the political use made of our most beautiful nouns, of the noblest intentions our language can express, degrades them until, at length, they become stale, worn, and exhausted. We know all too well what happens to these ideal values, these superior creatures of the abstract language and of detached thought, in the violence of debate, in the tragicomedy of party politics, in the agony of dissension. *Order, Reason, Justice, Fatherland, Truth, Virtue*: these august words, prostituted for factional ends, are shouted into the public ear, disgracefully bandied about and garbled by the ranters while the majesty of their venerable meanings is degraded by the cynicism of leaders and by the credulous simplicity of the led. As a result, great words, thus tainted, fall into disrepute and the man of integrity—above all, the man who thinks—will ultimately abandon them to their wretched fate; he shuns them as mere means of manipulating passions, of exciting men to behave in herd-like fashion. These masterly inventions of classical philosophy, of all philosophies the purest, come to a wretched pass; they are turned into deplorable weapons, into slogans and battle-cries, into instruments of a permanent civil war which is the chief concern of so many people. They are forsaken by thought. The statue that has become an idol requires the sacrifice of intellect, and this frequently involves a bloody sacrifice.

So it was that virtue, through these political profanations and many abuses, fell into disfavor and contempt. The dignity of this noble word, far from preserving it in the present age when language is tending more and more to become what we see it has become, places it apart, ostracizes it from life which grows increasingly positive in outlook, that is, increasingly ruled by material needs, by technical conditions whereby everything is organized in terms of number and fact, and with brutalizing effects. Today man is inclined to deny what he cannot define. On the other hand, it may well be a law of language that any word which has appeared too prominently in the social comedy, has duped too many people, and is itself compromised in too many self-seeking schemes will evoke distrust and bear the stigma of insincerity. From 1840 onward, the word *virtue* became suspect. It takes on a shade of ridicule. It seemed too good to be true on *modern* lips, for the nineteenth century felt it was modern and knew it was the nineteenth century. *Virtue* was tolerated, if at all, in administrative rhetoric and could still serve for Crownings of the Queen of the May, though these too were about to be taken over by vaudeville. Yet who would not have had misgivings about uttering this supremely pure word in the presence of wits such as Beyle or Mérimée? At the mention of virtue, these refined experts in the art of pretence might have been expected to prick up their ears (so highly sensitive to false notes) and cast a glance charging you with asininity or playacting. The fact is the middle of the last century was a crucial moment in the history of the elevated style, as in so many other domains. To judge the period by its books and speeches, one would gather that it discouraged men from openly declaring their loftiest sentiments. It was as if a kind of inverted modesty prevailed, allowing sensations, passions, and material concerns to replace more noble themes as the only fit subjects of literature, which justified its preferences by arguing that it sought on the one hand to record the mores of society and, on the other, to challenge aesthetic conventions.

Even crime, which had been tolerated only if it was dressed in the full regalia of tragedy and premeditated in Alexandrines often shabby but always proper, or which was relegated to the popular ballad and lurid pamphlets, crime now appeared in all its horror, speaking its native tongue on the stage as in literature. Drama and the serial novel caught the public's fancy, giving it the rudiments (more or less authentic) of underworld slang. I do not know whether there is any equivalent for *virtue* in that language.

Is it not remarkable that we can determine, almost to the year, the critical moment after which our word lost its currency everywhere but in the catechism and in jest, in the Academy and in light opera?

This observation can be reinforced by several others, all bearing on language. We are witnesses to the extinction of various words and locutions which at one time described or designated what were considered the best or the most valuable or the most refined attributes of man viewed as a moral being. One scarcely ever hears it said of someone nowadays that he is "upright"; *honor* itself is a thing of the past for statistics are not in its favor. Expressions like "an honorable man," "word of honor," "an insult to honor" are not only dying but are seemingly without substitutes in the language as it is currently used. I make a point of distinguishing *current* usage from what we, among ourselves, normally refer to as *good usage*: alas, the latter is little more than an Academic notion today.

I should not care, gentlemen, to attempt a kind of counter-proof at this point and, without pausing, see which words once thought base or infamous and thus proscribed from the conversation of polite society as well as from mentionable books, are now uttered very audibly and, on the whole, published with surprising ease. From time to time one can hear a startling specimen in literary drawing-rooms, and the theatre itself is often quite racy.

But I refuse to go even one step farther—that is, one step too far—in this investigation for fear that the cupola above, which has never echoed a coarse word, should fall on our heads.

My plan is simply to describe for you the strange progress of language evolving in a particular direction. It is as if modesty in speech has literally been *perverted*; discretion has switched topics: what formerly was praised dare not be spoken of in public, what was censored and veiled is now exposed unblushingly. Without being aware of it, we are witnessing, abetting, acquiescing in the mass desertion of words which directly translate the things once hallowed above all others. This desertion is, in my view, one of those truly historical phenomena that conventional histories never bring to light, accustomed as they are to seeing only the immediately visible, or even the traditionally visible, while the mind, provided it will not settle for predigested offerings and will use its capacity for surprise and its faculty of inquiry, has at its disposal a wide range of antennae which, directed toward documents and the observable world, record relationships and events imperceptible at first glance. Among those facts which contemporaries and participants are the first to overlook are the very ones that lie at the heart of any given epoch and distinguish it from those immediately preceding and following; the result is that their writings make no mention of the essential or do so only implicitly.

I wish to speak about the values a period decrees or finds itself inwardly compelled to adopt, about the hierarchy of these values in the public mind, about their influence on mores and social appearances, on the law, on politics, and the arts.

For me a period is well defined when I know what it prizes, what it depreciates, what it shuns, what it pursues and neglects, what it demands or tolerates, what its affectations are and its reticences. The body social has its leanings and its dislikes, its strengths and its weaknesses like all living organisms. But this system of tendencies and reactions in public feeling is subject to a kind of gradual mutation, so gradual as to go unnoticed, yet the attendant change of values represents an event of signal importance affecting all human relationships. We have, for example, seen a remarkable change within the last few years in the value of the idea of *political freedom*. At one time this was an all-conquering dogma while today it is almost a heresy, subjected to ridicule and even proscribed.

But for the present my subject is the value *virtue*. In order to define it without adducing information you could not verify for yourselves, I have kept to language, venturing to show only the self-evident so that your impressions will coincide with mine, and the same questions will occur to both of us, spontaneously, without my prompting you.

What then is this problem that comes so naturally to mind on mere consideration of the register of births and deaths among words? I would formulate it as follows:

Who are we? Or rather, *what* are we, we modern men who have unconsciously ceased using the name *virtue* or, for that matter, feeling any live response within ourselves to the august idea that this name powerfully evoked at one

8   113   v o c

time? Does this renunciation which I have tried to point out to you indicate a substantial change in man's moral being? Has this century, along with its many other egregious and often inhuman innovations, sponsored a revision so great and so despicable in what I would call the *ethical sensibility* of individuals, in the idea man has of himself and of his brethren, in the value he attaches to good conduct and to the consequences of acts, that we must conclude that the age of good and evil has completed its cycle, that vice and virtue are today no more than museum caryatids, symmetrical forms of a primitive mythology, and that scruples, altruistic acts, self-sacrifice are either outmoded graces, psychological curiosities, or complications and burdens which modern man cannot afford to have encumbering his existence, or cannot even fathom any longer, his mind is so trained on the measurable?

Moreover, it could be that some day certain contradictions will appear between our way of life, which is ordered by material powers that at once rule us as masters and serve us as slaves, and the requirements of old-fashioned conscience. Looking farther ahead, if our age were to evolve along present lines and lead to a total, definitive organization of society—which would presume that all minds had been molded according to some model adopted by the State— men would obviously need to invent a new set of values. Some acts we call *virtuous* would doubtless fall outside the pale; other acts we condemn would become morally neutral. It is even possible to imagine that in such a social structure, what we call *personal values* would lose all meaning, for ideas like egoism and altruism could no longer penetrate minds schooled to function as precise units of the organized community. And our traditional virtue, relegated to the status of a discredited myth, would be defined by the learned men of some future age as the spiritual energy that, several centuries before, had driven a few individuals to compensate with fine and generous actions for the vices of an inferior social order long since superseded.

What I have said, gentlemen, is not pure fantasy, nor even an especially bold premonition. I have kept within the limits of a world as familiar to you as to myself. In the largest countries on the surface of the earth, including one whose considerable population has, note this, fewer illiterates than any other, we can observe, in a spirit of curiosity not without amazement and consternation, the aggressive beginnings of a change unprecedented in scope and audacity. There have been scattered attempts to create a new kind of man, attempts predicated on various principles, for what they are worth. In some quarters work is worshiped, in others race, but both share an extraordinary will, which sometimes they forcibly impose, to upset moral evaluations hitherto considered absolute, to train the younger generations by a system that will prepare them for a society organized to the last detail. I should not be surprised if, within the next thirty years, the customs, the manners, the forms of social life practiced by half the human race underwent a change as radical as that wrought in the material world by the applied sciences.

Every political philosophy and ethical system is ultimately based on man's idea of himself and of his destiny. For centuries, the West has toiled to create the concept of personality. Slowly, laboriously, and sometimes painfully, it succeeded in investing the individual with civil, political, legal, and metaphysical value which it finally elevated to the status of an absolute, designating the latter by such conceptions, now considered banal and generally disparaged, as *liberty* and *equality*. But we no longer feel the impact of these famous words, words which should not evoke the idea of rights acquired once for all time and conferred on man because he is man, but rather of objects that must be constantly rewon, the rewards of a perpetual struggle waged not only in the social arena and on political grounds but first of all within and upon ourselves. This republican motto is in reality the definition of aristocracy. It presupposes the strength to be free and the will to be equal. These are virtues. When such virtues decline, facility takes control, freedom leads to disorder, and the will to be equal becomes indistinguishable from envy.

Today, however, our belief in the infinite worth of the individual, a belief ratified by the thinking mind yet constantly disputed by one's eyes and by life itself, is now in open conflict with the idea of the collective and the State that represents it. Our generation will live to see man depicted not as that sovereign value which took centuries to create, but, in large sectors of the world at least, as a fraction of the social system constituting the be-all and end-all of his existence. He serves the collective life as a mere means and is vouchsafed no independent value, for whether he gives or receives, his every transaction is with the community.

If, then, we no longer speak of virtue, is it not because this term must share the same fate as the idea of the individual considered as an end in himself? The word is vanishing from our new world along with the thing it signifies, and this world, once it has been thoroughly organized, will have no room, will provide no occasion for that uncommon power known as *virtus*, which sets certain people apart, buttresses them against the instinctual drives all of us possess, enables them to perform acts quite as original in the realm of the human heart as the works of an artist, and not merely original but often surpassingly beautiful and refined. What indeed could be more original than doing good with sensitivity? Is not loving one's kind a way of distinguishing oneself among them? But let justice triumph and society, under its sway, will have no further need for love. It is rather remarkable, gentlemen, that a question theologians once found deeply troubling—the old debate between justice and love—should now be springing to life again in a meditation on the present drift of human affairs. Is it not obvious that in a society so organized as to anticipate and satisfy our every need, there would be no place for charity or demonstrations of self-control? Besides, many constraints will have vanished along with the traditions that call for them, traditions that are nothing if not the observance of certain virtues.

It would seem that man is belatedly regretting the foolish choice he made in the Garden of Eden when he plucked the fruit that made him conscious of Good and Evil, rather than an apple from the Tree of Life, which would have given him immortality and left him to irresponsible pleasure. Perhaps Adam is beginning to act as though he had made the other choice. He would prefer henceforth to know nothing of Good and Evil.

This new-found ignorance—or growing indifference—betrays itself very clearly in many features of our social behavior that have only recently come into being. Our indulgent attitude toward many things that would at one time have given rise to scandal, our genial and all-inclusive tolerance, the fluent diversity of our relationships, the laxity we countenance in writing and on the stage, our tendency to use expedients in every sphere, not only in politics and commerce where they are perhaps inevitably the rule, but as if by contagion, in private life as well—none of this is calculated to reinstate the noun in question and the adjective that derives from it. . . .

Another thing: we have contrived a kind of philosophy from this moral state of affairs. Floating about in the psychological atmosphere of our age are a few abstract ideas, more or less misunderstood, which have a curious way of adhering to our easygoing sense of morals. The words *relativity* and *objectivity* are forever on the tip of our tongues; and we are becoming vaguely accustomed to believe that all things can be treated as phenomena, that for all things we can, if we search, find a fitting expression independent of the variables that influence the observer's view. But the inward events, the perceptions, the imperatives, the private games, the expectations, the likes and dislikes, the rewards and momentary pangs, the treasures of light, of hope, of pride, of freedom and, elsewhere within us, the hellish depths of madness, of absurdity, of error and anxiety that comprise our emotional life, this affective, unstable, and overwhelming universe, is absolutely dependent on him who perceives it. In this realm the phenomenon creates its observer and the observer creates the phenomenon; between them, as between the poles of a magnet, exists a perfectly reciprocal bond.

Gentlemen, I have a story to tell and this seems the appropriate moment. While straying through these thoughts that were devised for your hearing and seemed at every point to be leading far from my theme, I was startled from my digressions by the announcement that a visitor had arrived; scarcely was his name announced and not even grasped, than he was standing before me, bowing. This sudden stranger

had materialized in my presence quite as swiftly as a shaft of
light in a room when the shutters are flung open. At first I
was afraid he might be some early-rising candidate for the
Academy, or else a poet athirst for advice. . . .

"Sir," the intruder said, "I apologize for making such a
sudden entrance, but I cannot help moving at nearly the
speed of light. Let me explain: I am supposed to be carrying
out a survey. . . ."

"A survey?" I rejoined. "A survey? Sir, it's time you left.
No one is keeping you. You can put your alacrity to good
use by disappearing. A survey! Please include me among
those who are weariest of delivering oracles. In the course of
this past week, I have spoken a dozen times before thinking.
On one occasion, I was asked to name the most beautiful
line of verse in our language; on another, I narrated the
greatest day in my life; I offered opinions on State reform
and on votes for women. I even very nearly issued a pro-
nouncement on the comma! The truth is, my good man,
that I am past admiring my brain for all the wonderfully
various things it had no idea it contained. Strike it with one
word and a hundred others fly out like sparks."

"Sir," he continued, "I am making an inquiry into
virtue and it has come to our attention that you have been
assigned to speak on this subject before the Academy. Your
mind is doubtless boiling and fermenting with the theme.
Would you consent to impart a few of your thoughts to
me?"

"But what newspaper do you represent? Is it right or
left? I must formulate my answer in the light of yours, and
define the sort of virtue that suits your politics."

"I am sorry, sir, but nothing of that sort exists where I
come from. Everyone up there (or down there) is agreed

that there is one way, and only one, of deceiving and being deceived. Sides are irrelevant."

"But where in the world do you come from?"

"From far away, sir. I come from the densest star in the heavens, where a mere drop of water weighs about sixty tons by your measure and our brains are of the same specific gravity. I come, sir, from that singular star known here below as the *Companion of Sirius*. M. Ernest Renan created quite a reputation for Sirius, a place he seemed to know well. He brought back from there a certain *point of view* which was widely adopted in his time, but today human beings seem to have difficulty in adjusting it to their eyes. Your earth is quaking a bit all over and this famous point of view requires a very firm base indeed. . . ."

(These curious observations enlightened me. I began to suspect that here was one of those delightfully opportune creatures who used to pay providential visits to M. de Montesquieu and to M. de Voltaire whenever those admirable colleagues of ours needed the acute and preternatural naiveté to be astonished at seeing what everyone else saw with no astonishment at all. . . .)

"Aha!" I exclaimed, "I do know you after all, and that's where I have you. It is you who should do the talking. Undoubtedly you have just rounded the globe in a fraction of a second, prying into every nook and cranny. Come now, my good Mr. Special Correspondent, before dispatching your psychogram to the *Companion of Sirius*, give me the substance of it. Have you found virtue?"

"I am at your service, my dear sir," was this astute visitor's well-turned reply. "I consider it a great honor to be summoned to collaborate on a report destined for the Academy. But in my travels round your tiny spheroid, I have found very little on which to base a eulogy of virtue. I am well aware that noble acts are done in secret and have their origins in virtue. There is a great deal of light on earth, and feverish publicity reigns here. Light embarrasses and withers the good; noise puts it to flight, so that true virtue abhors the glare of day, to the extent of feeling ill at ease when practised too knowingly. I should think that the better one knows oneself, the more difficult it must be to believe oneself capable of a disinterested act. Whoever feels that he is doing good should, as a matter of obligation, feel a sense of shame or anxiety. Consider, then, sir, how many ways there are of casting doubt on the excellence of an intention, or on the purity of those motives that precede or follow a worthy gesture. Do you not find that of all those who do good, a sensible proportion vaguely believe that the good they do will magically ward off some evil, or else fancy that in performing a good deed they are paying dues on the advantages they enjoy, albeit apprehensively at times? Such people are not virtuous but superstitious."

"How learned you are in the ways of the human soul!"

"Heavens," the subtle one replied. "I have merely read your best writers. Have you noticed, Mr. Academician, that not one—I am referring to the really good ones—places any trust in the goodness of your species; and that the best take the blackest view?"

"That is because blackness is considered beautiful in literature. At first, virtue appears somewhat insipid, but that impression is soon dispelled and even reversed on closer scrutiny. Moreover, our great writers are all moralists more or less, which goes to prove that moralists thrive on evil. . . . But tell me, what did you observe during your world tour in search of virtue?"

"Your world is in a wretched state, my dear sir. When misery reaches a certain point, it becomes so hard to practice virtue that heroism is needed to do what ordinary virtue can accomplish under normal circumstances. Dare I tell you what I really saw? Everywhere I saw a host of thieves and assassins. . . . That is nothing new. But what struck me— and this will be the substance of my dispatch—is the enormous interest this vandalism elicits in all circles. Everywhere on your streets and in your public places one sees people— their noses pressed against sheets just newly blackened with ink—taking evident delight in all manner of crimes, as though the latter had been committed expressly to appeal to their ravening hunger for the new and more abominable. They are absorbed by the heinous crimes that run on from page to page, intersecting, joining, crisscrossing, some of them political in nature, others passional, still others motivated by money-lust but all of them interlarded with photographs of faces of which some could fit equally well the victim, the assassin, or the judge, and others often belong, not to them, but to some unfortunate *celebrity*, a member of royalty or of the Institute, a worthy centenarian pressed by the circumstances of the printed page into the midst of this sordid affair. . . . Little wonder the word virtue has fallen into disuse in your talk."

"Yes . . . I grant you that such ignoble curiosity does exist. But wouldn't you say that we are making marked progress on our tiny planet toward a generalized state of sincerity? A while ago, I was of two minds: it occurred to me that possibly we are not worse than before, but rather seem so because we present ourselves, such as we are, more truthfully, more nakedly before our own minds."

"Indeed," murmured the observer, "this past summer I

saw a crowd of Truths on your beaches, confronting the sun in the most sincere attire."

"The only thing is," I continued, "when I consult that imposing series called *The History of Hypocrisy through the Ages* (which has not yet been written, to be sure, but I postulate its existence and let my mind leaf through it), I begin to doubt that progress has been made after all. Besides, hypocrisy is eternal; it will last as long as there is some ideal, held in honor among men, which it pays to appear to serve. There is nothing more significant than the definition of Good in fashion at any given moment, serving as a useful guide for model behavior."

"That is why," the envoy replied, "I greatly wonder at certain demonstrations I observed during my world tour. It would appear that disciplined energy is fashionable. Almost everywhere there are cohorts, simply and rather oddly dressed, who have a habit of saluting, some with raised arms, others with their fists clenched. . . ."

"And did you find that this promoted or detracted from the cult of Virtue?"

"I didn't know what to make of it. At first it seemed to favor virtue, then, immediately afterward, to harm it. I thought it might favor virtue because constraint inevitably seems to strengthen the empire of the mind over the instincts, and thereby it may be Virtue. But then I began to wonder whether most men do not owe their magnificent discipline to fear, or to imitation, or to self-seeking pretence. And if men are trained this way, how does such an education differ from the training of an animal? Are these young creatures, these children, not reduced to living and thinking the life and thoughts prescribed for them? They will turn out to be precise instruments and powerful machines, but even if these instruments and machines were applied to some worthy task and made to serve only the Good, what would it matter to Virtue to be followed blindly, without even being chosen? For Virtue, the important thing is that in these people the mite of hidden, universal freedom belonging to man will have been destroyed."

"My good investigator, you are a philosopher."

"I don't know about that, sir. I see what I see, and I do my job. Besides, as I've already told you, I haven't been able to draw any conclusions. . . . What conclusions could be drawn from the chaos you have made, where good, evil, the absurd and the admirable, heroes, knaves, madmen, creators are thrown together and mixed in the general ebullition of an age which seems to have but one law: to drive this indiscriminate mixture to an ultimate point of confusion, incoherence and inner provocation . . . and what I say is vividly borne out on any of those sheets we referred to a moment ago. Confronted by this rampant disorder I scarcely know what to think of it, but thought is futile anyway since no image can render disorder, nothing in it permits one to fall back upon a past, to anticipate a future, to foresee, to construct and give shape to some plan. . . . Sir, I have interviewed the best minds in the world. Each one sees things according to his own lights and all these lights, when put together, shed total obscurity. Oh, sir, what a voyage! Almost everywhere I went, I saw abundance give rise to need, I saw stupidity and crime further their own ends with devices which it had taken a hundred men of genius to create. And what customs, what amusements! . . . So many inanities, so many causes for alarm! Never have there been so many baubles, so many threats, and grave ones at that! . . . Coupled with your elaborate systems of hygiene are perils of your own invention; they abound in your streets, in the air, in your games. . . . While millions of people are living on the edge of starvation, you burn, dump, and adulterate much of the splendid fruits of the earth. You conceive and organize the most rapid means of traveling through space, and at once you erect obstacles and barriers to stop the traveler; he is interrogated, watched, suspected; he loses a vast amount of time before he is permitted, for some reason that never comes clear, to enter a country no less wretched than the one he just left. The virtue of patience dies out in him. He curses the States, whose benefits he can perceive only after long reflection, whereas their power he can feel weighing upon him incessantly. . . . Of all the creatures in your world, States seem to me the least virtuous of all."

My astral reporter seemed thoroughly upset. I said to him: "What is the matter with you? What the devil did the State do to you?"

"Oh!" he said, "As for me—a mere shaft of starlight sent on a faultfinding mission—I am quite indifferent to taxes, red tape, turnstiles and barriers—the only signs by which a State can certify its own existence. . . . But while I was searching here and there for a few atoms of Virtue to make a small ingot, really solid and unalloyed, a mad sprite of an idea leaped into my head: to analyze the State for its virtue-content."

"A most unusual subject of research . . ."

"You must understand, sir, that in my land we admit almost no distinction between creatures ascertained by our senses and creatures of our reason; we accord to each the same degree of existence, or of non-existence—it little matters which Thus, virtue may be found not only in men and in women, but in all entities. It exists in literature, though not so prominently as it once did. There is some virtue in medicine, in geometry, and a good deal, I am sure, in the Academy, so that looking for some in the State was not such an outlandish idea. . . . Be assured, sir, that this has nothing whatever to do with politics. But just imagine what an appalling citizen we have in the person of a State. Here is truly an odd creature. Virtue, sir, virtue would be its ruination. It owes its life to the most marked contradictions. It practices nearly all the vices, covets what belongs to others, breaks all its promises, frustrates its creditors, sells opium, makes dogma of its injustices, recognizes only might, superior numbers, and results achieved with brutality. Ah, sir, there's a somebody you would never honor with the smallest Montyon prize. . . ."

"That would never have occurred to us. But for lack of States to honor, we have humbler organisms of the purest merit. In your tours and detours, was the Rue Xaintrailles in Paris part of your itinerary?"

"Rue Xaintrailles? Never heard of it."

"Yet we, who are far less agile, know it all the same."

"What's to see there?"

"There you will find a little house inhabited by a group of admirable women who call themselves Dominican nurses of the poor. They spend their time ministering to the poorest and most afflicted people in the most wretched and sinister quarter of Paris. There is not much respect for anything in that neighborhood, where poverty and degradation have made men as brutally materialistic as money; when they have it to handle, it will make them beasts of prey. Yet these ladies are revered, and gratitude shows in every glance as they walk through the street."

126

"Allow me, my dear Master, to note this down. But you are laughing. . . ."

"No, my friend. I am doing more than that. I am jeering."

"Well then would you mind telling me whether this laugh, or jeer, is meant for your humble servant?"

"But for whom could it be meant?"

"But what have I done to you?"

"Nothing. You make me laugh. See here, my dear Very Special Correspondent; you have circled the earth and I have not left my room. With the most piercing ray, you have passed into human beings, analyzed minds, weighed designs, appraised values without being much the wiser for it. I have not budged, yet find myself surrounded with more than enough virtue to frame an address for the Academy. Wait . . . admit that you have done a very bad job of conducting your inquiry. Have you so much as heard of a society called the Shelter, whose work is concerned with homeless people? Or another, of very special interest to us literary people, called the Widow's Mite? Have you, my dear Sir. . ."

"A moment, Sir. Give me time to write this down. You were saying, yes, the mite of widows of literary men . . ."

"And the Children's Welfare, and the Federation of Seamen's Guilds and the Catholic Association of Young Women and . . ."

"Not so fast, my dear Master."

"And above all, do not forget Mlle. Maire. . . . She is a teacher of drawing. For forty years she has devoted her life to the blind, and especially to the blind whose health is frail. She cares for them, feeds them, dresses them, entertains them, tends the graves of their dead, and, what is still more admirable, teaches them to take care of one another. In this instance, charity becomes a virtue that ultimately requires all the gifts of a human mind. The heart invents, devotion prompts the imagination, and the intelligence uses all its resources to soften the lot of those poor blind people, and to guess their smallest needs."

"I am ready to confess, my dear Master, that the *Point of View of Sirius* does not account for everything. . . ."

"I could show you many more things. . . . You see, there is, after all, nothing quite like an old Academy to reveal perfection not encountered on the streets. Do not forget that the best things are always rather hidden, and whatever is highest and most precious in the world is always open to denial."

"Farewell," said the Reporter. "I'm on my way to the *Companion of Sirius*. But directly I get back up (or down), I shall begin a campaign to found an Academy. We shall have but forty times sixty thousand seats, which will make two million four hundred thousand elect, and leave five or six billion hopefuls."

Address to the Congress of Surgeons

Gentlemen,

I AM HERE in this deservedly celebrated amphitheater because a few of you are my friends and the rest of you are ready to be indulgent. I feel not only the strangeness of being here at all but also alarm and embarrassment at having to address you.

To begin with, of course, I have a few simple duties to perform, as agreeable as they are obvious. My opening gives me no qualms.

First of all I wish to thank you for the honor you have done me; the ritual nature of those thanks in no way detracts from their genuineness. What could mean more to a man whose occupation is entirely intellectual in nature, and whose works, since they lend themselves to no factual verification or justification, have no ascertainable value, than to receive this evidence of esteem from you, gentlemen, who know something certain, who accomplish something positive, and who subject everything you think and do to the pragmatic test of its consequences? Your profession is one of the most complete ever known; it demands the development and devotion of the full man. My profession—if it is one—obliges me to specialize in the pursuit of a few shades.

Now you would be startled if I failed in my second duty of assuring you that I am utterly unversed in the field of surgery—as though you were not even more keenly aware

9   129   V O C

of that fact than I am. In almost any field, what the ignorant man knows least is his own ignorance, for he has no means of measuring its extent or plumbing its depths.

Having now expressed my gratitude and established my incompetence, I cannot go on without paying tribute to the constantly growing power of your art, the signal merits you display as artists, and the benefits you bring to mankind, benefits that often could more aptly be called miracles. The masterpieces your hands have wrought are the only ones I know whose worth shows itself in two contrasting ways: they command the admiration of connoisseurs, and they inspire thanks and blessings from many others.

All this constitutes the easiest part of my task, yet I say it with all my heart and feel it, believe me, far more strongly than I can say.

Having pronounced these ritual words, hesitating on the threshold of my own silence, what can I go on to say to this gathering?

What can I tell you that has something to do with surgery, since you are surgeons; and has nothing to do with it, since I am not. There is a precise problem.

Surgeons are people accustomed to every kind of revelation, and if they are not satisfied, they go in search of the truth where they can find it. Their eyes and hands probe the pulsing substance of our beings. To lay bare the body's distress, to find the affected flesh, beneath the most dazzling of outward appearances to discover the worm that gnaws within—here is the essence of their task. This being the case, of what use would it be to try to hide anything from them? Why not simply confess the ideas that come to me even if they belong to those disjointed thoughts one tries to winnow out when one can, in order to construct a discourse whose clear structure and pure style may give an impression of formal and intellectual perfection?

I began by wondering why you have adopted the remarkable custom of bringing a non-surgeon to the platform of a Congress of Surgeons. Perhaps you regard it as a kind of live experiment, a form of intellectual vivisection? Or perhaps you think it may be useful, or at least interesting, for dedicated specialists in a field whose potentialities and limitations they know full well, to bring into their midst a well-meaning individual who knows no more about their activity than the next man, and to ask him just what kind of idea he has of their science, of their art, and of them as practitioners.

The answers of this lay person must, by definition, be valueless. But I am not sure that his remarks, provided they are artless enough, might not be highly suggestive to the learned minds that hear them. Whenever one explores any distance into the delicate structure of an intensely absorbing scientific discipline, one almost necessarily loses sight of certain elementary difficulties, of certain initial conventions which an ingenuous bystander may usefully bring up again for unexpected attention.

You call on this bystander, who resembles me closely enough for me to speak for him, to explain to you what meaning he attaches to the words *surgery* and *surgeons*.

"Well," he says, "that all depends on the circumstances. ... Sometimes it is a science, an art, a profession that comes to mind. But sometimes those words suggest more than anything a form of pathos. You are the most enterprising servants of the will to live. But you make us shake in our boots as well. The eyes drawn to yours both fear and wish to read your thoughts. It is your strange lot to inspire dread and spread salvation. The idea of surgery is probably less terrifying than it once was; a hundred years ago an operation was still a kind of bogey, the last resort if it entailed cutting into the inner organs rather than merely an amputation or the basic cleaning and care of a wound. At those moments, only extreme urgency and desperation precipitated an operation. Since that time surgery has developed immeasurably in power and audacity, in technique and results; the frequency and safety of operations have deeply changed people's attitudes. The remarkable progress you have made has not gone unnoticed. If history paid a little more attention than it does to these matters that touch life directly, it would take note of this shift in people's thinking. Moreover, these advances in your art can have considerable effect on the lives of the principal actors in history. The famous grain of sand lodged in Cromwell's urethra could be quickly removed today. And Cleopatra's nose would be looked at in very simple terms of plastic surgery. If that baneful beauty had been slightly disfigured, the face of the world might have gained a little in the process.

Now any simple act of reflection will always cast a look toward the past, toward what it conceives as the root, the seed, the first appearance of whatever is. In thinking about the immemorial origins of your art, and setting aside the science it has become, an ingenuous onlooker may wonder if it is not the development of a kind of instinct, if it does not arise from that natural impulse that makes us want to get our hands on the pain that we feel, to employ on ourselves the same actions we use on things, in order to modify the afflicted part of our body, treating it as though it were an unknown enemy. If his sense of pain did not stand in the way, man would probably mutilate himself with some frequency. That is an instinctive defense mechanism, one that attains the perfection of an automatic reflex in certain living creatures, whose injured or captive limb amputates itself and falls off of its own accord.

You have carried to the extreme point of precision and audacity this impulse to act directly on the seat of disease or evil and to go at it armed for the kill. There is something strange about thinking of such an action applied to a living being. Who knows if man's first notion of biology may not have been just this: *it is possible to cause death*. Thence the first definition of life: life is a property that can be obliterated by certain acts. Furthermore it normally sustains itself only by devouring itself in a vegetable or animal form. A veritable torrent of life is perpetually swallowed up in the abyss of other life.

But if there is one form of natural action that destroys life and becomes criminal when consciously organized to that end, fortunately human genius conceived of and created another opposing action. Man learned to combat that same death he can produce and spread with such dangerous power; as a counterpart to the wound that causes death, he dared open the wound that could save life. Surely it is one of the boldest of all human undertakings, this penetration and direct modification of the body's tissues. Surgery no longer hesitates to enter the most noble and delicate of our organs, and it has no fear of its steel in the brain, the heart, the aorta: that is, in organs whose time is so precious that a fraction of a minute lost by one of them can bring about the loss of the whole being.

Thus by your hands and in order to save life, one type of human action has developed in complete opposition to the very different process and well-nigh inconceivable process of natural growth. Our actions normally consist of distinct acts applied to an external matter according to a very variable plan or model. In certain cases those successive acts can be separated by intervals of time without affecting the result. On the other hand what we call *Nature* produces phenomena by continuous development and progressive differentiation. *Matter, making,* and *form* cannot be separated in Nature; a living system does not refer us to distinct variables, and our analytical grasp of things, which discerns and manipulates what we call *time, space, matter,* and *energy,* appears to be incapable of forming an exact idea of such vital phenomena. Nature, for example, never gives to the different parts of living creatures the degree of freedom we give to those of our mechanical devices. She remains ignorant of the wheel; every animal is formed of a single piece. And she has never created an animal that can be taken apart. This inferiority on the part of natural manufacture has obviously had important consequences: to it we owe most of our progress in surgery. It fell to the lot of you surgeons to apply our intelligence, industry, and inventiveness to repairing the living sections of an individual. It is unquestionably an action against nature, but to which nature gives a good chance of success, enough to make your work possible. She consents to knit back certain tissues—to heal flesh and reform bones. Yet we are less fortunate than the holothurian, which can jettison all its viscera at once and grow a new set at will.

But your work as surgeons must combine various mechanical means with the uncertain ways of living substance; it must find a balance between *making* happen and *letting* happen and refrain from disturbing the sensitive equilibriums that separate life from death; and it must consider the reactions and emotions of the individuals concerned. For all these reasons, your work probably takes account of a greater number of independent variables and conditions than any other human activity. Your calculated boldness, which is so often successful, requires that all the most diverse and rarely associated qualities be assembled and coordinated in a single man. I think often of all the capacities that your day's work must alert in you, ready to move from potentiality into action, from an unexpected problem to a decision, from decision to execution, always under pressure of time, or of moral and social considerations, or of feelings. Then comes the act itself: under your fingers the particular case takes the place of the textbook problem, reality comes to light in the raw, confirming or refuting your diagnosis and examinations. There the unexpected crops up, discoveries that can be troublesome in varying degrees; new decisions to be improvised and acted upon immediately.

All this demands so rich a combination of talents, so quick and well-stocked a memory, so sure a technique, so steady a character, so great a presence of mind, with physical stamina, keen perception, and precision of movement, all so far out of the ordinary, that the coincidence of so many different qualities in an individual surgeon suggests the kind of improbable creature whose very existence we would do well to doubt.

And yet, gentlemen, there you are. . . .

Now you understand that someone who knows only what everyone else knows about you cannot, when he thinks of you, help picturing you in the dramatic performance of your art. Today this takes place in a semi-religious solemnity, surrounded by an opulence of polished metal and white linen, all bathed in a shadowless light emanating from a crystal sun. A citizen of the ancient world called back from the grave to see you going about your serious task, robed and masked in white, with a marvelous lamp affixed to your forehead, flanked by attentive acolytes, performing, as if according to an elaborate ritual, on a creature plunged in magic sleep and laid open under your gloved hands, would believe himself a witness to who knows what sacrifice, one of those celebrated only among the initiate of the ancient sects. But is it not the sacrifice of disease and death that you celebrate in this strange and cunningly staged ceremony?

Let me note in passing that this liturgical appearance, like a mystic or symbolic operation broken down into acts or stages and organized as a performance, has grown up naturally around the real operation on living tissue because of the need for rigorous discipline required by asepsis. She is a jealous goddess, whom the Greeks and Romans would surely have personified; they would have built shrines and worshiped her in some way. Asepsis: that is the banishing of all contamination, the creation and preservation of a certain *Purity*. How can one help thinking here of the immense role the idea of *Purity* has played in all religions, in all ages, and of the development it has undergone following a parallelism between cleanliness of the body and that of the soul? Pasteur gave the idea a whole new meaning. . . .

This consideration might help us understand the nature of certain rites still carried out today though their practical value has disappeared.

But, as I said, I have never seen a surgeon officiating; I doubt if I could bear the sight—a fairly common weakness. I know that more than occasionally a young medical student is affected by the spectacle of an operation, to the point of feeling faint and having to leave the room. This flinching is one of the most mysterious of our reflexes. I remember having seen a child scarcely three faint at the sight of a few drops of blood from a harmless cut received by the person who had brought him out to play. That child had no idea of the tragic meaning of blood; and the person concerned showed no feeling but irritation at having stained her dress. I have never been able to understand that event. Possibly one should not look for any explanation of such things. One can always furnish a verbal interpretation of those cases of extreme sensitivity and create the illusion of understanding. But I see no purpose in piling up illusions and taking unfair advantage of our many devices for *thinking we understand.**

By definition, of course, this kind of shock never affects you surgeons. You live in the midst of blood, and moreover must be constantly at grips with anxiety, pain, and death, the most powerful stimulants to our emotional echo chamber. The critical moments, the extreme conditions of other lives fill every day of your life, and in your steadfast spirit the exceptional event, however distressing it may be to the persons concerned, takes its proper place among statistics governing the same category. You shoulder the heaviest of responsibilities at the most urgent and delicate of moments.

In the eyes of the witness I have tried to represent to you, all this makes you extraordinary beings, standing apart from the rest of us, more to be admired than understood.

But I shall make bold to go a little farther in analyzing the wonderment you cannot help arousing. And perhaps I shall go a little too far. . . .

* Since writing this text, I chanced on the following passage in Restif de la Bretonne: "The sight of blood made me fall in a faint, *even before my reason had given me perfect understanding of what was being said around me." Monsieur Nicholas.* [P.V.]

Yes, if the figure of the surgeon inspires such admiration in me, because of the concentration in one person of all the qualities indispensable to his art, there is still something else in you that astonishes me, a completely different matter, less generally noticed perhaps than the other traits I have brought out. I find myself confronted by a certain enigma concerning you when I come to think of you as human beings and simply that—I mean in your non-surgical life.

Must I come to the point of speaking my mind fully? Dare I try to lay open the surgeon himself? But, since I have you here, how could I resist the temptation of this biopsy? In any case, I shall not venture too far where my curiosity leads me; I shall make the incision, and close it again.

As surgeons you bear magnificently the weight of everything I have mentioned—severe, poignant, terrible burdens fraught with perplexity and emotion. You also bear the weight of your knowledge. You have constantly in your possession a precise knowledge of the innermost forms, the structure, the very springs of the human being. But nothing could be less human.

This being can no longer be for you what it is for the rest of us who have no such knowledge. It does not represent for you that sealed vessel, sacred and arcane, where life is preserved in secret ways and external actions mysteriously take shape. We live on without having to know that living requires a heart, inner organs, a whole labyrinth of tubes and filaments, a living stock of retorts and filters, which make us a perpetual theater of exchange between different orders of magnitude of matter and different forms of energy, from atom to cell, and from cell to visible and palpable masses of tissue. All this equipment within us betrays its presence only through the disorders and pains it produces now and then, breaking through to consciousness at one point or another, and thus interrupting the normal flow of our functional ignorance of ourselves.

Functional—I say functional, referring to the ignorance of simple mortals concerning their own bodies. I apologize for borrowing the imposing term, with uncertain results, from a vocabulary I have no right to. It suggests, I think, that our ignorance of our internal economy plays a positive role in the accomplishment of certain functions which are not, or are only slightly, compatible with a clear conception of their action, functions which respond to stimulation only if our intelligence is paying no attention to them. On occasion a particularly conscious or self-conscious person has to distract his mind in order to accomplish an act that must happen by reflex or not at all. And under the circumstances a strange thing happens: the consciousness and the will *favor* the reflex action, counter to the mind's tendency to observe any phenomenon and thus impede the natural course of things.

There are, after all, certain functions which prefer dark to light, or a half-dark at least—a minimum of the presence of mind necessary and sufficient to prepare the ground for or trigger their action. Under the threat of failure or paralysis, they require that their cycle of sensitivity and potency be completed without observation or interruption from start to physiological limit of the act. This jealousy or modesty of our unconscious processes is a remàrkable thing. One could extract a whole philosophy from it that could be stated thus: *At one moment I think; at another I am.*

The mind must not poke its nose into everything, even though it has assumed that vocation. You might go so far as to say that it is for external use only. The rest, our basic internal functions, are classified as secret. That secrecy is essential, and we might even measure the vital importance of our various functions according to their incapacity to tolerate conscious attention. In order to live, let us ignore. . . .

But how can one ignore the mechanism of life when one does nothing but observe it, manipulate its parts, study its workings and its changes? At times I have wondered how the knowledge you, as surgeons, possess of the organism, the images you carry of its most hidden regions, the constant contact, familiarity even, with those parts that are most reserved and for the most emotive ends, can avoid thwarting your natural being, the one in which an occasional uneasiness must occur, and in which ignorance, or rather functional innocence, is needed to permit the vegetative soul to find the shortest line of action—to follow its *world line*, to borrow a term from theoretical physics.

But my question is purely theoretical as well. The fact of your lives supplies answer enough. Everyone knows that nature and knowledge are perfectly compatible in the person of the surgeon. Your intellectual and technical inhumanity comes to terms very happily with your human-ity, which is often compassionate and tender. Your existence reveals a near-perfect harmony among knowing, doing, and feeling, between living and understanding, between lucid self-possession and the final surrender to that innocence I called, whether correctly or not, functional.

Therefore the problem does not exist. But the miracle does, and it is not the only thing we find to admire in a surgeon.

Of necessity there is an artist in you. I am not speaking of the kind that produces works of art with a brush or a pen or a chisel. It might be well to say something along those lines and point out the benefits of exchange between two activities which have many things in common.

But here I am speaking of your own art whose material is living flesh and which represents the clearest and most striking case of the immense and stirring spectacle: the action of man upon man.

What is an artist? More than anything else, someone who carries out his own thought, thought which can be realized in several ways. Therefore his personality plays a role, no longer at the purely psychic level where the idea takes shape, but in the act itself. The idea is nothing in itself and costs nothing; one must act on it. If the surgeon is to be considered an artist, it is in so far as his work is more than the impersonal execution of a series of gestures. An operating manual does not make a surgeon. There are I believe several methods of making incisions and suturing, and each one has its points. That is to say surgery has several styles. Of course I know absolutely nothing about it—yet, I am sure of it.

All the knowledge in the world will not qualify someone as a surgeon. Only the Doing can establish his claim.

The very name of your profession proclaims the importance of *Doing*, for Doing belongs to the hand. Expert as they are in incisions and sutures, your hands have to be just as skillful in reading by touch so that the tegument becomes transparent under palm or finger, and they must be able to sketch what they have touched and explored far inside the dark cavities whence they withdraw.

Surgery, chirurgie, manuopera, manœuvre, handwork.

Every man uses his hands. Yet is it not significant that

since the twelfth century the term *œuvre de main* has been restricted in meaning until it refers exclusively to the hand-work that serves to heal?

But what is there a hand cannot do? When I began thinking about surgery, with the present occasion in mind, I found myself meditating at length on that extraordinary member in which almost the whole power of humanity resides and which strangely separates humanity from the rest of nature, even though nature produced it. We need hands to change the course of things, to modify bodies and force them to obey our most arbitrary plans. We need hands not only to construct the simplest invention, but even to conceive of one intuitively. Remember that among all animal species there is probably none but man capable of tying a knot; and this act, easy and everyday as it may be, presents such difficult problems for intellectual analysis that the most subtle techniques of geometry are needed to solve, however unsatisfactorily, the problems it poses.

It also takes hands to create a language, to point out the object named, to mime the action of a verb, to punctuate what is said.

But I shall go farther, and say that a profoundly important relation must exist between our thought and that marvelous complex of properties secured for us by our hands. The slave increases his master's riches, and does not confine himself to mere obedience. Just consider our vocabulary of the most abstract words. Among terms indispensable to mental activity are many which must have been furnished by simple hand movements: *to put forward, to take, to grasp, to hold, to seize, to place.* Then again: *synthesis, thesis, hypothesis, comprehension, supposition. . . . Addition* refers to giving; *multiplication* and *complexity* to folding.

That is not all. The hand has its own philosophy. Long before Doubting Thomas it was a sceptic. What it touches is real. The real has and can have no other definition. No other sensation produces in us so great a certainty as the resistance of solid matter. The fist striking the table seems to wish to impose silence on all metaphysics, as it imposes the idea of will to power on the mind.

I have sometimes wondered why we have no *Treatise on the Hand*, a thorough study of the innumerable potentialities of that miraculous machine which blends delicate sensitivity and nimble strength. There would be no limit to such a study. The hand brings a countless number of instruments to serve our instincts, our needs, our ideas. How could one ever describe this device which, at the proper time, may strike down or bless, receive or give, feed, swear allegiance, beat time, read for the blind, speak for the dumb, reach out toward a friend, and be raised against an adversary? It serves as hammer, pincers, and alphabet. Can it do more? Such lyric variety should be enough. This *universal agent* is successively instrumental, symbolic, oratorical, calculating. Might one not call it the *organ of the possible*, just as in another way it is the *organ of absolute certainty*?

Thus the hand distinguishes itself from all other organs capable of doing only one thing. One of those capabilities brings to mind a notion particularly associated with surgery.

Surgery is the art of performing operations. What is an operation? It is a transformation effected by a series of distinct actions performed in a given order in view of a well-defined purpose. The surgeon modifies the state of an organism. He touches its very life, he intervenes in the sequence of life, but with such great orderliness and precision of movement that his action takes on a strangely *abstract*

143

quality. Just as the hand distinguishes man from other living creatures, the ways of abstraction distinguish the procedures of the intelligence from the modes of transformation in nature.

At this point, gentlemen, allow me to use my imagination; the poet has a moment's license to appear.

I can imagine the extreme astonishment, the stupefaction our organism must feel when you violate it, when you suddenly expose all its palpitating treasures to light and air and introduce steel instruments and constraining forces into its remotest depths. Thus you produce on this inconceivable living substance so foreign to us (and which is ourselves) the shock of the outer world. What a blow! What an encounter!

Is this not at the same time an instance, a telling image of what goes on in every part of the modern world? Everywhere we can see the devastating effects on man himself of the very techniques he has created. He lives under perpetual shock. What will become of that tissue of relations, conventions, and notions that has slowly developed through the ages, and which, for some ten years, has been submitted, or rather has submitted itself, to the test of the superhuman and inhuman forces that man has learned to summon? Our eminent Chairman spoke to us a moment ago of the rapid changes in therapeutic science, which he could explain only after describing the particularly critical state of the physical sciences in general. It seems to me we might put it this way. We have acquired a vast reservoir of indirect knowledge, which reaches us through relays and informs us through signals about events taking place in orders of magnitude so far removed from those having some relation to our senses, that all the notions by which we normally conceive of the world no longer hold good. All scientific imagery has been declared bankrupt. On the new scale of things, the concepts of particle, position, time, matter, energy become virtually interchangeable. The very word *phenomenon* loses its meaning, and perhaps language, no matter what system we adopt, cannot avoid introducing error into our minds through its substantives and verbs. Even number is disqualified by its very exactness. It will have to fulfill the new role of substituting probability for any definite and identifiable plurality.

In other words, our direct picture of the world is riddled and blurred by various forms of indirect information that reach us from the recesses of the infinitely small. No doubt they add a great deal to our knowledge and power; but we understand less—perhaps less and less. That is the effect of the *relay*. By means of a relay a child, with his little finger, can set off an explosion or a fire completely out of proportion to the effort he expends. A scientist, using modern means of manipulation through relays, can produce results that he will interpret by saying that he has exploded an atom. But he will have to admit that the expression is only a makeshift, and that the term *electron*, for example, has no other meaning in the positive sense than the system of devices and movements necessary to produce certain phenomena observable by our senses.

Therefore our science can no longer aspire, like the science of yesterday, to a structure of converging knowledge expressed in laws. A few formulae, people used to think, ought to be able to contain all our experimental knowledge, and an ultimate scheme showing the relations of equilibrium and transformation, comparable with or identical to the equations in dynamics, ought to be the true end of scientific investigation.

But the increase of new techniques has so multiplied the number of available facts that science finds itself modified by its own action on itself, changed in its very purpose. It is constantly forced to modify its theoretical foundations in order to maintain a kind of workable equilibrium with all these new facts, which increase in number and diversity with its means. An ordered summation of knowledge, which used to be the basic goal of all research, is no longer conceivable. Theoretical science breaks down into partial theories, which are indispensable and admirable tools, but *tools* nevertheless to be picked up and put aside, and whose value rests entirely on their usefulness. It follows that any contradictions these theories may display among themselves no longer constitute essential weaknesses.

All this amounts to a profound modification of ideas and values. Knowledge is henceforward dominated by the power to produce effects.

You must forgive me for taking advantage of your courteous attention for so long. You are as good patients as you are surgeons. I have run over all the limits—not only of time, but of discretion for a literary man speaking to scientists. We writers believe we know something, though we are at home only in the universe of words. Few people in the world compare with your Secretary General, who wields a scalpel, a pen, and a crayon, and displays an elegant style with those three pointed instruments. You saw how skillfully he grafted a collection of honors and merits onto this unworthy Honorary Chairman. . . .

I should have confined myself to saying that surgery as it is practiced today strikes me as one of the most noble and absorbing aspects of the extraordinary human adventure as it has been speeding up and intensifying its scope over the past few decades. Grave symptoms confront us on all sides in our fellow creatures and in the events we live through; I am not the one to say what deliriums, what insidious infections, what manic-depressive cycles they may signify. If one feels only too often like the witness of the last moments of a civilization that wishes to end its days in a luxurious orgy of destruction and self-destruction, it is a good thing to turn one's attention toward a group of men who sift through new discoveries, methods, and technical innovations in order to find and use those elements that can be applied to the saving and the comfort of their fellow men.

II

The Future of Literature

I DO NOT know whether what we call literature is to have a future, nor whether the extraordinary transformation of human life and of the mind's ways of communicating with other minds will permit any further development of books, nor whether the resources of language will continue to be used to stimulate men's thinking. Perhaps language will be replaced by other ways of reaching people's sensibility and intelligence? We may already wonder whether a vast, purely oral literature will not very shortly replace the written literature familiar to us. I allude to radio broadcasting, which now is spreading to all parts of the world. Moreover, the process of recording images and transmitting them over great distances is also likely to modify human relationships that were formerly based on writing. One can imagine a work, for example, in which the descriptions have been supplanted by direct, plastic representations and in which feelings are conveyed by recorded sound more or less musical in nature—thanks to what might be called the potential omnipresence of music from recording apparatus and transmitters.

In short, there is nothing to prevent us from imagining that literature as we know it may become an art as archaic and as remote from everyday life as geomancy or heraldry or falconry is today. Perhaps in a century's time there will be only a few scholars left who can painfully decipher our written characters and, after long critical effort, reconstruct the state of mind of an age when written language was the principal means of preserving and transmitting thoughts and impressions.

In order to conceive the possibility of such a change, or rather, in order to cite developments that support the sinister prophecy I have just made, it is enough to observe the evolution of literature over the past few centuries. Literature is an art founded on the *abuse of language*, on language as a creator of illusions as opposed to language as a transmitter of realities. Everything that makes a language more precise or exaggerates its practical side, every sacrifice imposed on it to obtain easier and more rapid transmission is contrary to its function as a poetic instrument. In all nations the common speech is increasingly infiltrated with foreign words and with the technical language originally developed for the use of science and industry. Moreover, all forms of rapid communication based on language tend to reduce the number of complex forms; and in most cases the vernacular is already markedly different from the literary language, which comes to resemble a classical tongue, almost a dead language, taking its place alongside Greek and Latin. So, as the vernacular becomes daily more technical and more international, increasingly reduced to a system of signals and abbreviations, it tends to exclude the nuances, the exuberance, the rich vocabulary, the intricate turns of phrase which allowed ancient authors to vary their writing through a wide range of styles and to use a wealth of resources that might be called ornamental. It is possible that humanity may henceforth give up exploring that forest of symbols in which the great image-hunters of former days, such as the Biblical poets or the subtle "bird-catchers" of Persia, pursued and captured metaphors, those combinations of figures with which they burdened and decorated their poetic edifices.

That is not the end of it. All literature is dominated by the nature of the audience to whom it is addressed. Every book is aimed at a reader who corresponds, in the writer's mind, to the idea he has of his contemporaries. In effect, there is a kind of law of supply and demand in literature. Readers of a given era get the quality of literature they want, in keeping with their culture and their powers of attention. Now, modern man is, in general, an execrable reader. The time has gone forever when a man could sit down with a book and enjoy spending the entire night by the light of a single candle searching out its guiding principle and mastering the work's innermost meaning and at the same time savoring the finest details of its form. And if readers have neither the time nor the patience to weigh and appreciate the words given them to read, authors will no longer choose their words with care and affection. Cultivated people are already satisfied with slipshod reading. They devour newspapers and works of passing interest without paying the slightest attention to the form in which they are written. In such writings their minds find only raw information or momentary distraction, with the result that in more and more cases they are satisfied with random statements, unproved assertions, pronouncements of an almost brutish crudity. All coordination of form, everything that requires sensitivity and sustained attention has vanished.

We must not forget that the great majority of people today, caught up in the machinery of a fearfully clockwork day, can perforce give only a limited amount of time to reading. Moreover, this short period is of a very special kind. Most people have an average of fifty minutes a day to give to *reading for pleasure*. This is a scant hour when placed against the enormous contemporary production of "literature." This meager hour is necessarily devoted to newspapers rather than magazines, to magazines rather than books. It is taken up with publications all the more widely read for being loosely put together; by definition a newspaper is composed of more disparate data than a magazine and even more so when compared with a book. During the hour they can devote to the freest and what ought to be the most refining cultivation of their minds, therefore, most people are victims of a routine in which disparateness and distraction are the rule. Furthermore, this short interval is usually spent in one of those vehicles which large cities have imposed on our daily lives. Reading is done in the train, the trolley, the subway, or the bus, and the works necessarily tend to be such as can be read in conditions of movement and chaos. It can be seen that I have no great illusions about the future of literature as an art which may reward the deepest study.

The foregoing considerations may or may not be challenged, but I think that this way of looking at the state of literature has at least one advantage: it tends to make us consider the existence and evolution of that art in its relation to the functioning of life at a given period. Literature may not have been sufficiently considered in this light, and perhaps we might do well to begin a whole study of its development, its greatness, and its periods of weakness, by examining first of all not the works themselves as they have been preserved but rather the conditions under which they could or might be produced.

Such facts as the amazing increase of literacy during the

last century in all countries have had an incalculable import-
ance in the production of written works. I am convinced that
a thorough analysis of the consequences of this increase
would lead to unexpected conclusions. In particular, it
seems to me very likely that the development in Europe after
1852 of a tradition of recondite, difficult, stylistically man-
nered works, incomprehensible to the general public, is
related to the growth in literacy. A kind of compensatory
mechanism seems to have come into play, and those rare,
refined, and inaccessible works were needed to counteract
the enormous expansion of the literary field and the intensi-
fied production of mediocre works which had resulted from
this development.

This development can be compared to a rather different one
to be noticed recently: the growing interest of the public in
works of a philosophic nature. It can be said that the extra-
ordinary proliferation of purely impressionistic works, or
those of pure imagination—that is, novels and stories—
has brought about an unconscious reaction in a great number
of readers who have turned to what seems to them a less
arbitrary occupation for their leisure time. It is well known
that works of a somewhat abstract character find readers
more easily today than thirty years ago. And, on closer
examination, it would be easy to show that the same thing
has already happened, to some extent, in the domain of
imaginative literature itself. The novel, which in its earliest
forms is a narrative meant to transport the reader into an
imaginary world having the appearance of reality, a kind of
literary *trompe l'œil*, and which in the form of wonderful
adventures, love stories, stories of crime, etc., has played such
a part in the mental life of humanity, has for some time been

handled in a different way (often very successfully) in a spirit quite remote from fantasy. An attempt has been made, over and over again, to redeem, as it were, the purely *sumptuary* character of works of the imagination by introducing *didactic values*. Novelists have prided themselves on their insights into sociology, or it may be psychology; at times they have wanted to use the results of scientific research, or they have aimed at influencing people's religious convictions. However, quite apart from such special tendencies, the creation of the realistic novel was simply the expression of a desire to diminish the proportion of arbitrary invention in works where the arbitrary, the imaginary, is nevertheless the essential ingredient—and at the same time to refit real experience into the fictive products of the imagination.

I sometimes catch myself thinking that the role of literature in the future will be close to that of a *sport*.

Let us exclude from our consideration of literature all uses of language now being rendered obsolete or ineffective by the direct expression of things, by the new media's direct impingement on our senses (movies, *omnipresent* music, etc.).

Let us also exclude a whole range of subjects (psychological, sociological, etc.) in which any freedom of treatment is now becoming difficult because of an increased precision in those sciences. Literature will then be left with a private domain: *symbolic expression and imaginary values*, as they arise from the free combination of the elements of language.

Just as new sources of energy and new mechanical devices, by reducing our muscular activity, have allowed, or rather forced, us to create *pure* uses of our bodies, to develop them more *harmoniously* through *games* than was ever permitted by backbreaking or constrictive physical labor, so the complex function of language may reach a similar liberation.

In that event, we are living through an awkward phase of this remarkable function and a critical age for the art of words.

The Centenary of Photography

THE ACADEMY, invited to take part in this ceremony marking the centenary of a truly French invention, indeed one of the most admirable to emerge in the course of the nineteenth century, could not fail to pay its own respects to our great compatriots who hit on the principle of photography and were the first to fix an image of visible objects by employing the very light those objects reflect.

We, however, are a Society devoted particularly to the cult of Letters, which at first glance show no obvious affinity to photography, nor do they appear to be more affected by it in spirit or practice than by many other modern products of human ingenuity.

We all know that drawing, painting, and the imitative arts as a whole were able to exploit this power of a sensitized plate to capture forms instantaneously. Directly the process of fixation made it possible to study, at one's leisure, beings in motion, a great many errors of observation came to light: the renderings of certain artists, persuaded that they had caught a horse's gallop or a bird's flight, were proved, by this means, to be utterly fanciful. Thanks to photography, the eye grew accustomed to anticipate what it should see, and to see it; and it learned not to see nonexistent things which, hitherto, it had seen so clearly.

Yet, this possession of the means of reproducing natural and living appearances through a simple transformation of physical energy seems to have had no certain effect on Letters nor to offer them any marked advantage.

On the contrary, this marvelous invention might—or so it would seem at first—ultimately restrict the importance of the art of writing and act as its substitute rather than help enlarge its scope or enrich it with valuable insights. It is a very largely illusory claim that language can convey the idea of a visual object with any degree of precision. The writer who depicts a landscape or a face, no matter how skillful he may be at his craft, will suggest as many different visions as he has readers. Open a passport for proof of this: the description scrawled there does not bear comparison with the snapshot stapled alongside it.

Thus we might be discouraged from making further efforts to describe what photography can automatically record, and we must recognize that the development of this process and of its functions has resulted in a kind of progressive eviction of the word by the image. In fact, it is as if the image, in published form, has been led, by its overweening desire to steal the place of words, to steal some of their more irritating vices as well—prolixity and facility. I might add that photography even makes so bold as to practice an art in which the word has, from time immemorial, specialized: the art of lying.

So it must be agreed, then, that bromide proves stronger than ink whenever the mere presence of things suffices, whenever the thing speaks for itself without benefit of proxy, that is, without having recourse to the wholly arbitrary transmissions of a language.

As for myself, I see no harm whatever in this, and am strongly inclined to believe that it might in a way benefit literature. I mean that the proliferation of photographic images I mentioned could indirectly work to the advantage of Letters, Belles-Lettres that is, or rather, Letters that truly merit that adjective. If photography, which is now capable of conveying color and movement, not to mention depth, discourages us from describing, it is because we are thus reminded of the limits of articulate language and are advised, as writers, to put our tools to a use more befitting their true nature. A literature would purify itself if it left to other modes of expression and production the tasks which they can perform far more effectively, and devoted itself to ends it alone can accomplish. It would thus protect itself and advance along its true paths, one of which leads toward the perfecting of language that constructs or expounds abstract thought, the other exploring all the variety of poetic patterns and resonances.

Let me remark here that when photography first made its appearance, the descriptive genre in Letters was becoming an all-invading fashion. The background and outward aspects of life figured almost disproportionately in works of verse and prose alike. Between 1820 and 1840, this background was, on the whole, imaginary. There grew up around landscapes and 'forms a romanticism whose cavalier treatment of people as well as objects was inclined to total flights of fancy; it invented an Orient and a Middle Ages cut whole cloth from the sensibility of the period, with the aid of some small erudition.

And then came Daguerre. With him, the photographic vision was born and it spread by singular leaps and bounds throughout the world. A marked revision occurred in all standards of visual knowledge. Man's way of seeing began to change, and even his way of living felt the repercussions of this novelty, which immediately passed from the laboratory into everyday use, creating new needs and hitherto un-imagined customs. Now everyone had his portrait done: a luxury once reserved for the privileged few. Traveling photographers scoured the countryside. Not one event in human existence went unrecorded in some snapshot. No marriage was complete without a picture showing the couple in wedding dress; an infant was scarcely born—a few days old—he was brought before a lens; decades later the man he grew into might stand amazed and affected before the photograph of this baby whose future he has used up. Every family kept its album, one of those albums that allow us to revisit the past: portraits that we find touching in retrospect, apparel that now seems quaint, moments in time that have become such as they were, relatives, friends, and people we do not recognize, who played some essential or random role in our lives. In short, photography laid down a real pictorial record of the social life. If he had lived a bit longer, Balzac, who searched tombstones and signboards for unusual names to give his countless creatures, would surely have found in these archives of faces an excellent stimulant to his genius.

But with the advent of photography, and following in Balzac's footsteps, realism asserted itself in our literature. The romantic vision of beings and objects gradually lost its magic. The scenic backdrop showed itself for the canvas or cardboard it was. A new imperative held sway, requiring that poetic invention stand clearly apart from any narrative claiming to represent reality. I do not mean by this that the literary system of Flaubert, of Zola or of Maupassant owes its formula to the advent of photography, since I dread searching for causes in a realm where they cannot fail to be found. I am doing no more than take a snapshot of an era.

It is far from certain that objects close together on a photographic plate have anything in common beyond their nearness. The more we are tempted to see some underlying connection between the phenomenon called "Realism" and the phenomenon called "Photography," the more we must beware of exploiting a coincidence.

The Empire of Letters is not, however, limited to the provinces of Poetry and the Novel. It extends into the vast domains of History and Philosophy, whose vague frontiers sometimes disappear altogether where they border on the territories of Science and on the forests of Legend.

It is here, in these vague regions of knowledge, that the coming of Photography, or the mere idea of it, acquires remarkable and specific importance for it introduces into these venerable disciplines a new condition, perhaps a new uncertainty, a new kind of reagent whose effects have certainly not as yet been sufficiently explored.

History is a narrative to which we apply what will distinguish it from mere storytelling. We invest it with our present energy and whatever fund of images we can draw from the present. We color it with our likes and dislikes; we also construct systems of events and, to the extent that our heart and power of mind permit, we give a kind of life and substance to people, to institutions, to incidents, and to dramas bequeathed us in documents as mere verbal outlines, and often bare ones at that. For some people, History amounts to something like a picture-book, an operatic scenario, a stage performance, or a series of generally critical situations. Of these tableaux, which our mind creates and then submits to, some depict wonders, enchantments, theatrical effects too beautiful to believe, which we sometimes interpret as symbols, or poetic transpositions of real events. For other people, whose interest takes a more abstract turn, History is a catalogue of human experiences to be consulted much as one would consult meteorological records, in the identical hope that the past will divulge something of the future.

The mere notion of photography, when we introduce it into our meditation on the genesis of historical knowledge and its true value, suggests this simple question: *Could such and such a fact, as it is narrated, have been photographed?*

Since History can apprehend only sensible things, being based on verbal testimony relayed through words, everything on which it grounds its affirmations can be broken down into things witnessed, into moments that were caught in "quick takes" or could have been caught had a camera-man, some star news photographer, been on hand. *All the rest is literature.* All that is left consists of those components of the narrative or of the thesis that originate in the mind and are consequently imaginary, mere constructions, interpretations, bodiless things by nature invisible to the photographic eye, inaudible to the phonographic ear so that they could not have been observed and transmitted intact. As a result, any discussion about the causal value of certain facts, about their importance and their meaning, revolves around non-historical factors: they are the ventures of our critical or inventive faculties, more or less controlled by documents.

I leave out altogether the problems of authenticity. On this point, however, photography teaches us new reasons to be cautious. Prior to its invention, any fact, provided a sufficient number of people swore that they had seen it with their own eyes, was considered incontestable. Not one court of law, not one historian would not have accepted it, even if reluctantly. Yet, just a few years ago, a snapshot was proof enough to demolish the testimony of some hundred people who swore to having seen, with their own eyes, a fakir pull himself up a rope that he had just cast into the air where it hung, miraculously suspended.

In any event, the natural outcome of these reflections would be a sort of Philosophy of Photography, which might in turn soon lead us back to Philosophy itself, if this digression did not threaten to take me outside my competence, my present assignment, and the limits set by the object and the occasion of this ceremony.

In a few words, I shall give a cursory idea of what a philosopher might have to say if he turned his thought to this invention of ours.

Photography could, for example, prompt us to revive, if not rejuvenate, the ancient and difficult problem of *objectivity*. That little story of the fakir goes to show that the awkward and somewhat desperate solution of eliciting testimony from the few, in order to establish for all mankind a thing's objective existence, was easily destroyed by a mere sensitized plate. It must be admitted that we cannot open our eyes without being unconsciously disposed not to see some of the things before us, and to see others which are not there. The snapshot has rectified our errors both of *deficiency* and of *excess*. It shows us what we would see if we were uniformly sensitive to everything that light imprints upon our retinas, and nothing else. Thus it might not be impossible at least to limit, if not to abolish, the classic problem I mentioned, by ascribing objective value to every impression whose replica, whose likeness, we are able to capture—impartial light being the only intermediary between the model and its representation.

But there are other, very intimate and very ancient, affinities between light and Philosophy. In every age, philosophers—the theorist of knowledge and the mystic alike—have shown a rather remarkable predilection for the most commonly known phenomena of optics, very often making use of them, and sometimes subtle use, to picture the relation between consciousness and its objects, or to describe the illusions and insights of the mind. Many telltale expressions of this remain in our vocabulary. We speak figuratively of clarity, reflection, speculation, lucidity, and ideas; and, when trying to express abstract thought, we avail ourselves of a whole visual rhetoric. What could be more natural than to compare what we take to be the unity of our consciousness, complementary to and as it were the opposite of the variety of our knowledge, with the source of light which reveals the infinite multiplicity of visible things, each individually formed out of myriads of solar images? The blue of the sky is created by countless mirrors whose smallness we can compute. Moreover, the vicissitudes of light among bodies can give rise to any number of effects which we cannot resist comparing with the states of our inner sense of perception. What has proved most seductive to thinkers, however, and furnished the theme for their most brilliant variations, are the deceptive properties of certain aspects of light. What would become of philosophy if it did not have the means of questioning appearances? Mirages, sticks that break the moment they are immersed in water and miraculously straighten out when they are withdrawn from their bath, all the tricks that our eye accepts have figured in this memorable and inexhaustible enumeration.

You may be sure that I shall not neglect to mention here the most celebrated of all such allegories. What is Plato's famous cave if not a *camera obscura*, the largest ever conceived, I suppose? If Plato had reduced the mouth of his grotto to a tiny hole and applied a sensitized coat to the wall that served as his screen, by developing the rear of the cave he could have obtained a gigantic film, and heaven knows what astounding conclusions he might have left regarding the nature of our knowledge and the essence of our ideas . . .

But is there any emotion more deeply philosophical than the one we experience as we anxiously wait—beneath that rather diabolical red light which turns a glowing cigarette into a green diamond—for the emergence to visibility of that mysterious *latent image*, on the exact nature of which Science has not yet made up its mind?

Little by little, here and there, a few spots emerge like the first stutterings of awakening consciousness. These fragments multiply, cluster, form a whole; and, watching this configuration as its disparate elements, each one trivial in itself, proceed by leaps to form a recognizable picture, we cannot but think of certain precipitations as they occur in our minds, of memories that come into focus, of certitudes that suddenly crystallize, of the creation of certain rare lines of verse that fall into place, abruptly wresting themselves from the chaos of our inner speech.

All in all, can one think of a subject more deserving of the philosopher's meditation than the enormous increase in the number of stars as well as in the number of cosmic radiations and energies whose record we owe to photography?

Such breathtaking progress would, on deeper consideration, seem to suggest a truly odd prospect. Will it not be necessary henceforth to define the Universe as the simple product of whatever means we have at our disposal in a given era of bringing within the human ken events that are infinitely various or remotely distant? If the number of stars should strictly depend on whatever methods we invent to compute and number them, and if we reckon the future in terms of recent achievements, then it could almost be said that the numeration of the Universe is a function of time.

These prodigious results ought to make us think with special feeling of the continual efforts, of the countless experiments, of the self-denial and perseverance of inventors. I am thinking of the researches carried out under the most straitened circumstances, of the haphazard tools they themselves improvised, and the loneliness of their speculations. But, even more than this, what commands my respect is the disinterestedness that makes their glory complete. And their glory redounds upon the nation.

A Personal View of Science

AT MY OWN risk I mean to set down here what I make of *Science* in its present state, and where it seems to be going.

If history were a systematic discipline that followed a clear policy about the relative importance of the events it records, it would teach us, I believe, that the most far-reaching development in the period 1789 to 1815, the *development most laden with consequences affecting our own lives*, is probably not the great traditional drama of history constituted by the Revolution and the Empire. One can speak of the importance of an event only in reference to the role it plays in a person's life, and only in so far as that person is conscious of the role. Consequently the most important event of the years 1789 to 1815 is the invention of the battery and the discovery of the electric current by Volta in 1800.

From ancient times up to 1800, scientific observation and the analysis of its results had always been applied to *the same phenomena*.

Of course, the earth had become round, and then been endowed with various motions. Satellites of planets had become visible; unknown plants and animals had been discovered in newly explored regions. But this new knowledge did not modify one bit the substance or the nature of man's age-old experience of the physical world. Kepler's and

Galileo's and Newton's laws went no farther than formulating as yet unnoticed measurable relations between well-known elements of the world. In fact, the admirable simplicity and impressive success of these laws led people to believe that nothing new was to be expected that was not already implied in their formulation. Even major discoveries like that of the circulation of the blood, which came so surprisingly late, and the remarkable calculation of the velocity of light by Roemer in 1675, had no immediate consequences. Furthermore, the prevalent idea of science implicitly excluded the possibility of unforeseen occurrences.

In this state of mind and of science one could speak of a Universe and a unity of nature without having doubts about what one was saying. There was a unique Time, Space, Matter, and Light, and a sharp distinction between life and the inorganic world. And also, as demonstrated by science's subsequent triumphs in its aim of embracing and formulating the entire order of sensible phenomena, there was the magnificent structure of Dynamics with its general equations. Every object and event seemed due to find its place in that system.

In short, the expression ALL-KNOWLEDGE, as the counterpart of UNIVERSE, seemed to define a clear and possible ultimate. Laplace could imagine a mind powerful enough to conceive or deduce from a finite number of observations all possible phenomena, past and future.

I emphasize this point because my chief purpose is a discernible contrast, a contradiction between yesterday's notion of science and the notion now emerging.

The history of science amounts to a history of the ideas

169

people have had about man's power over things and about verifying those ideas. In its early stages this history has a set of double entries: in the one column, *magic* and in the other, tested *procedures*.

But this simple notion of a verifiable power of action upon things remained hidden for a long time (and is still so in many minds) behind the rather vague notion of KNOWL-EDGE I was speaking of—a kind of intellectual capital which, though always to be considered as subject to enlargement, must move indefinitely toward the ideal state of a structure of deductive propositions. This magnificent ambition amounts to imposing *a priori* on what we call the UNIVERSE a kind of unitary structure, not unknowable but, rather, conforming in some measure to our knowledge, and suggesting the image of all the visible heavens reflected in a polished steel ball.

The very word UNIVERSE requires the idea of a set of things grasped and graspable as a unity, of a continuity everywhere consistent with itself. Of necessity it raises problems of ultimate origin, conservation, and destination.

Between this UNIVERSE and its representation in a body of KNOWLEDGE, there was assumed to be a virtual if not real relation of *similarity*.

This is the splendid prospect and noble ideal that the "new facts" in their unforeseen and abundant variety and frequency now seem to condemn.

As soon as the electric current had been discovered, experiments began to reveal a number of phenomena of which no one until then had had the slightest inkling.

The era of NEW FACTS *had opened.*

They began to accumulate in a form of progression that

was as full of incidents as an adventure story. Science advanced by a series of accidents, and more than once the whole business of putting Nature on trial had to be begun again.

Electricity turned up everywhere, seeped into chemistry, invaded optics, transmitted itself through the void, and shook the foundations of our concepts of space, movement, matter, and light. The domain of physics expanded with startling rapidity: polarization, spectrum analysis, and much more. The nineteenth century closed with the discovery of X-rays and the first publication of the Curies on a new radioactive substance contained in pitchblende.

I shall not attempt to enumerate the discoveries that have been made since then in chemistry, astronomy, and biology, all ever in closer collaboration with physics. This rich harvest can no doubt be traced to the fact that almost every finding brings with it not only a new set of problems but also new procedures and techniques which are seized upon for immediate practical application. In the industrial spirit of the time their uses multiply rapidly, and the exploitation of each new discovery adds to the scientist's arsenal even more powerful and penetrating weapons.

But all these tools of metal and glass, all the experiments and observations, even when employed under perfect material conditions, do not suffice to bring about the true understanding of phenomena. They have to be reduced to their most significant expression, to their most useful and suggestive form. Only mathematics affords the possibility of transposing *real acts* of measurement and numeration in the world of bodies into *intellectual acts* of universal application.

During the seventeenth and eighteenth centuries, the discipline of mathematics had developed enormously. Calculus was discovered. But since the *era of new facts* was beginning for mathematical minds also, for what Pascal called the *esprit de géométrie*, the creative imagination, which had heretofore played a fairly restricted role, took on new importance. Of course the men who developed algebra and infinitesimal calculus had not been lacking in either insight or ingenuity; but it was their successors who carried creativity in the abstract disciplines, boldness and magnitude of concepts, far beyond their foreseeable applications. Quite apart from the immense progress made in established fields, a complete new symbolism grew up and became all but indispensable to research in physics. On the other hand, both in contrast to and in close and necessary connection with these new techniques for dealing with new problems, there occurred in mathematics a pronounced movement back toward its foundations and first principles. This reversion was accompanied by an almost excessive investigation into the validity of definitions and into the order and independence of axioms and postulates, by a sustained analysis of the notion of operation and order. All this resulted in the acquisition of the formal processes essential for the study of the new "reality" in its growing complexity.

But this reality is forever eluding us. Scarcely has theoretical thinking reshaped itself to receive the latest discovery than it seems some mischievous spirit throws out a completely new revelation that upsets or discards the whole mechanism of understanding just put together. Every experimental advance devalues a theoretical construct, and whatever suddenly enlarges our factual knowledge just as suddenly shatters the organization of our knowledge. Nothing illustrates this strange and significant conflict between observation and reflection better than the history of those "Laws of Conservation" which have not been conserved. After Descartes, Quantity of Movement yielded to Kinetic Energy, which yielded to Energy, and that in turn to Action. Mass itself has been found guilty of instability.

In biology the theory of evolution has already lost its erstwhile authority.

If I pushed this line of thought to its logical conclusion, I should state that all splendidly sweeping theories will finally be considered no more than devices of evident usefulness but precarious authority, with a claim to no more than a transitive value. I would be inclined to regard the idea of evolution, for example, as an attractive and fruitful construct of mind, but one which seems to represent the mind and its leanings toward continuity more than it does nature.

We are in for still more. Logic itself is taking a turn toward the unpredictable. It is being invaded and complicated by a new kind of subtlety. Algebraic notation has swept traditional logic off its feet and opens up the field of "relations analysis." Moreover the difficulties and surprises encountered in the realm of physics force the intelligence to worry less and less about the coherence and rigor of its symbols and their manipulation. One begins to sense that the goal is less to construct a system than to master a problem. Several different modes of reasoning can be used concurrently as tools, each fulfilling a particular need, and which do not have to be brought into perfect harmony with one another. Probability calculus alters the accepted meaning of natural laws. One can now debate at length the various methods of numbering plural entities, and the introduction of "quanta" or indivisible units of energy assigns a leading role to whole numbers in a universe that used to be the domain of continuity. That magnificent invertebrate we call the Theory of Relativity had just reached its peak of generality and flexibility when Quantum Theory came along and broke its spell. Still, they now exist side by side, helping one another like old friends. This monstrous and indispensable pair constitutes one of the strangest features of the pandemonium which is modern scientific thought.

The greatest of the recent difficulties and surprises I am referring to arise from the very nature of the newest of the new facts. These facts do not register on our senses; we suspect their presence because of other events which transmit these imperceptibly tiny disturbances, either spontaneous or provoked, into the scale of our perceptions. We do not know this absolutely inaccessible realm except through a system of *relays*. I say "absolutely" because even our imagination draws back at the prospect of a domain where the idea of form has no meaning, where the categories of judgment no longer hold, and to which we nevertheless refer in terms of objects and acts. In reality, to speak of *electrons* means to speak of a collection of devices which make a set of visible marks produced by an utterly imperceptible source whose existence is taken for granted as if it were a moving body. But it turns out that other traces of this hypothetical body will not agree with the idea we have a bodies and their movements. Now in biology, if we want to study the most intrinsic processes of cellular tissue, we must use relays, not only the microscope, but also a set of dyes and reagents whose effect is to kill what we wish to observe alive and to combine the object under scrutiny with an indispensable chemical agent that permits observation.

This knowledge through relays reminds us a little of

what happens in the formation of dreams: the brain of a sleeping man reacts to any local stimulus by transforming it, and produces what will give this isolated disturbance of sleep a cause and a development that both indicate and disguise the initial and still inaccessible event.

In short, we must recognize that as a result of increasingly powerful or sensitive instruments, the unpredictable has to be regarded as permanently incorporated into the realm of science. Everything suggests that the swelling number of "new facts" is attributable to these instruments; in other words reality in the scientific sense is a kind of "function of time," whose fluctuation has been astonishing if one compares the 1700 model of the universe with that of 1800 and then with ours today.

What is ordinarily called "science," meaning an exploratory or demonstrative account of things, is thus subject to a perpetual accommodation, which becomes even more difficult the more one strives to secure the unity of knowledge and of nature. To work out the theories of general relativity and of wave mechanics demanded immense and remarkable intellectual struggles. Serious consequences for the future of science arise from the fact that these profound and complex theories can be understood only at the price of mental exertion equal to that of their authors in working them out; and yet the same theories remain vulnerable to attack from any newly discovered facts. The problems become more and more complicated, and still must be rapidly solved so that theoretical knowledge, in its effort to unify, can keep abreast of the proliferation of facts, which in turn are a function of instruments.

All this leads inevitably to an extensive "transmutation of values."

First of all, our idea of the sensible world is altered. It used to be composed, as we conceived it, of a series of orders of magnitude fitted one inside the other; all bodies contained smaller bodies. Geometric and mechanical similarity was carried over from one level to the next. Statistics applied to numerable objects whose position and movement could be reckoned. All this now seems to vanish, and the assimilative faculty necessary to imagine and understand what we cannot directly perceive fails us. It expires in the nucleus of the atom. At this point everything starts afresh. Debatable probabilities replace isolated facts, and the very principle of identity (without which thought cannot exist) must be challenged. Thus everything changes radically in the depths of the infinitesimal, and those dwindling orders of magnitude turn into a set of Chinese boxes in which each world is less comparable to ours than the last.

In short, our means of investigation leave our means of comprehension far behind.

As a result the entire verbal, theoretical, and explanatory segment of our knowledge becomes essentially provisional. An unexpected experimental result or a more accurate measurement may be enough to change a constant into a variable, an element into a cluster of isotopes, a force into a property of space.

These circumstances have brought about a kind of depreciation of the speculative side of scientific knowledge, for it appears to have reached the limits of human understanding. Theories succeed one another, fade away, and become more and more closely identified with instruments or with devices that hardly survive a fleeting need or a vogue; and the very name of *science* is gradually changing its meaning. My purpose here is to draw attention to this change.

What do we mean today by the word *science*? It is closely associated with the idea of a kind of *credit*. All the fluctuations I have just referred to, the unpredictability of new developments, the diversity and even the divergence of methods of reasoning and proof, all this rocks that single unified intellectual structure we hoped we were building. The totality of observable events apparently refuses to condense into a universe.

But in compensation for this dwindling of the credit that was once attached to that original and splendid concept, we now have an increased power of action. Scientific knowledge separates into a *face value* that is collapsing, and a value redeemable in *gold*, a real, growing, and incorruptible value which can no longer be diminished by the same mental effort that created it.

Science then comes down (if it is a question of down) to a set of statements prescribing certain *steps* to be taken to obtain certain results. Any normal man provided with proper instructions and the necessary materials can perform these steps.

Formula for solving a problem; formula for preparing a certain carbon compound; formula for observing at a given time a particular celestial event; formula for suspending consciousness for an hour ... Such instructions, once known, are ours for good. Whatever technical vocabulary is used, whatever theory is in fashion, this value holds good and appreciates. A proven formula, a gold standard, the only science now is action. *Science is the complete set of formulas that always succeed:* DO THIS AND THAT WILL RESULT.

The *rest*, however, that perishable residue, remains for some the most precious element in research, the part most worthy of arousing the passions of the mind. While the end product of science may properly be formulas for action, *the process of creating science itself* is like the *creation of art*. Even if the value of science as knowledge and its thirst for knowledge lead no farther than the value of power and thirst for power, and even if science culminates in an impersonal, infallible, and therefore almost inhuman manual of operation, nevertheless, it is the attendant elements of illusion, ambition, faith in the expanding intelligence, which bring so much excitement into research with all its uncertainty, into the formulation of hypotheses and the difficult demonstration of the very thing one is most convinced of. If science is justified in moving toward greater *economy of thought*, it must expend along the way, and to good effect, a great excess of mental energy. If the abundance and variety of "new facts" disrupt the hope of raising a monument to physical nature, the universal temple resting on the once dreamed-of ideal laws, of beautiful simplicity, the very restlessness caused by perpetual novelty harasses the scientist and prevents science from disintegrating into a steadily growing mass of technical detail.

I said at the very beginning of this little study that the most important historical event between 1789 and 1815—according to my definition of importance—was the invention of the battery. But that event only set the stage for another, which may be the most important that has ever occurred: the invasion of all life by science, producing an active knowledge which is transforming man's environment and man himself to an unknown extent, with unknown risks, hopes, and prospects. No despot ever established authority over his subjects' most vital and intimate functions to the extent science has done in affecting every aspect of our lives, measuring us, and reducing us to statistics, bringing powerful new agents to bear on our senses, tending to substitute its language for our own, pervading our thought with objectively defined ideas. Such predictions are too easy to make; there is no need to go on. They can be expressed in a few words: *Science is a matter of effective action* (as I have been trying to show). This science, this growing control of things, deflects life away from its initial conditions of survival and conservation. Will life be able to withstand this "shift of equilibrium"?

In effect, life is becoming the object of an experiment in which the stakes are unknown and whose continual purpose is experiment itself. Our curious species fends for itself in the midst of uncertainty, torn between what it is, what it believes itself to be, and what it may become—three undefined ideas all contained by the opposing forces of its destiny. It looks as if man must be forever in search of a definition of himself. He has reached the point of finding in empirical science a path that is carrying him away from what he thought he was, with no deviation or turning back, and leading him he knows not where. Man is an adventure.

My Theaters

I RARELY GO to the theater and almost never to the films. This is not a credo, nor a matter of principle. It is merely a fact, the result of my peculiar sloth combined with some indifference to pleasures arranged on a fixed day at a fixed hour for large gatherings. Pleasure must have an element of improvisation and invention. No doubt films have much that is praiseworthy, but they make me feel that they are doing the work of invention instead of me, and in spite of me. In this sense they verge on dream, but dream oddly infiltrated by reality and, in a way, vitiated by it. The fleetingness of a film, the disjointed action, the true-to-life landscapes and obviously sham props, the absolute ease with which scenes can be changed, the sea, love affairs, whole days appearing and disappearing in a flash, and all this jumbled together as incoherently as associations of ideas—with the result that there is no depth, no duration, no substance, and nothing more stays in my mind than on the screen. Therein, perhaps, resides the simple secret of its universal appeal.

Furthermore, it answers perfectly to the aim or the compulsion of watching ourselves living. There is a story Stéphane Mallarmé used to tell, in amazement loaded with irony, of having watched a show in some London music hall that drew large crowds every evening. The management merely hired a family to spend their evening before the public, exactly as they would at home. They drank tea, chatted about the things they had done that day, discussed household matters, and possibly aired some of the topics they had read about in the newspaper: the gist of life itself. Afterward, everybody went home to bed satisfied. And why not? I am certain that a film whose scenario recapitulated the most uneventful day of the most prosaic person alive, simply showing him pursuing his life from morning till night, would be successful. Moreover, it is instructive to see, played out in ten minutes, what takes us twelve or fifteen hours of consciousness to do. I am not saying that *everything* need be photographed! Perhaps it may eventually be possible to do with man what has, I believe, been done with certain insects, and project his inner workings onto a screen. We would thus acquire a more accurate and perhaps rather dismal view of ourselves. Nature has refused us that knowledge of our organism, which we have acquired only by breaking into it. Then, too, seeing our organs monotonously at work, seeing the natural and acquired mechanics to which our whole existence may be reduced, might impel us to develop, in that region of our selves which the camera cannot photograph, a thirst for higher values, and for whatever would rid us of the feeling that we are *a serial product*, that we *live on a production line*.

I shall probably call down upon myself the wrath of all those people who are entertained, deeply moved, enriched by films. But I protest that I have never in my life sought to wean people from their sources of pleasure. I am not the sort who would try to convince others to dislike what they like and to like what they dislike. I have spoken my mind about motion pictures, but as one who is far from unaware of the art and craft that goes into a well-made film. I believe I know what it costs in experiment, groping, retakes, to attain these magic reels, and the idea alone of this labor, *as labor* of invention and realization, is enough to elicit my profound respect for this kind of production. I have often stated— and it is a true confession—that in any work of art, what interests me the most is what I can conceive of its craftsmanship. At times I am even tempted to make a film.

As I said, I rarely go to the theater. But a certain kind of theater often comes to me, and starts me dreaming: it is the recurrent object of my stray thoughts. And they are truly stray, for I gladly let them wander in the magic forest of the Possible, meaning the impossible, incapable as I am of keeping my mind on a track that would lead it to create a playable drama.

Among the many imaginings and useless ideas that beset me when I am thinking of the theater, two eminently simple conceptions polarize my mind, which travels back and forth between them, taking pleasure in emphasizing the opposition between the two. They are haphazard constructions, as idle as can be, but their incongruity and their way of recurring make me wonder at times if they aren't of some significance. When the mind at leisure goes about creating in its own fashion without any effort, devoid of any goal, it forms certain creative patterns which may have some hidden necessity and cannot be reduced to gratuitous games of chance.

I can imagine, then, two kinds of theater, one suggestive of a temple, the other of a Punch and Judy show (I say *Punch and Judy show* to simplify matters). With the latter I associate a hall, a stage, and scenery that are as obviously *theatrical* as possible: everything about it smacks of pasteboard, of painted plaster, of simulated gold; yet this system is somehow touching, cynical, exquisitely poetic in that it admits its incapacity for the true and despairs of attaining it, all the while confident that the illusion will work because everybody present wants it to: actor, author, public, even the prompter in his box. On the boards, which are real boards and wonderfully springy, life would burst forth with all the power to win over the spectator by the intense and infectious liveliness of the action, the startling dialogue, the dazzling repartees (sometimes due to the inspiration of the actor whose memory is fortunately unreliable). Here, then, we have the stimulus to make a spectator reel or spin with the whirl of impressions. Only the theater can create this immediate warmth and spontaneity. That is what I find missing in films. A photographic image forcefully evokes the past; and *it shows that what it shows no longer is.* One has the vague feeling when looking at these things that they are not being done now, but were done before they came into being. They are the "already-lived" trying to live again. Even the voices have a posthumous ring. My Punch and Judy show, on the other hand, retains some of the charms of "becoming." The actors, however often they repeat the same play, are forced to live anew what they are performing even for the hundredth time. They bring all of their living presence onto the stage, and notwithstanding their obligation to repeat the same role, they put before us characters who are more real for being freer than the inflexibly identical phantoms flashed upon the screen.

But when I have reflected long enough upon this theater as spirited and mobile as the mind, its freedom of movement, its variety of tones and situations, its momentary brilliance or charm, lead me to conceive or compose—as though in harmonic response or in refutation—that other theater which

I likened before to a *temple*. This one is governed by a kind of superior convention allowing no freedom whatever. Every movement seems regulated by laws as majestic as those which the ancients ascribed to their simple and grandiose universe. They believed in a world-order, and perhaps it was this marvelous misconception that imbued their art with the qualities we see in it of sacredness, of purity, of fatality, with that absoluteness characteristic of things that are complete in themselves, that do not crave notice but, at most, seem to deign to demand our eternal contemplation.

This theater would not be built of boards, but of more noble material. The interior would be subtly modulated so as to abolish the harsh contrast between stage and auditorium common to most theaters, where the curtain rises upon the spectacle of a totally different world, which charms us into adopting, temporarily, another life than our own. But on the contrary, the dramatic order I am imagining would have the very different purpose of invoking our deepest self-awareness, our *cosmic sense*.

The reader will perhaps have understood by now that I am thinking of a kind of *liturgy*. I cannot elaborate here the ideas I have long had in mind that would explain this conception. Many years ago, I spoke about them to Debussy, and offered him a brief outline of a work which would be based on it. Nothing came of this, but I had the opportunity, later on, to write a libretto as close as possible to my quasi-liturgical aims, when I collaborated with Arthur Honegger in the creation of the "melodrama," *Amphion*.

Unfortunately, the conditions under which this work was performed were such that the experiment proved meaningless. All that survives of it is an admirable solution to one of the most precise and exacting of musical problems.

On Phèdre as a Woman

AFTER READING *Phèdre*, or seeing the theater curtain fall,
I am left with the idea of a certain woman, a sense of the
beauty of the verse; a future reserve resides in me in these
durable effects and values.

The mind resumes its normal course, which is a riotous
stream of sensations and thoughts, but unknowingly it has
selected from the work the elements that it will henceforth
treasure among its supply of ultimate standards and criteria
of beauty. It never fails to single out, unconsciously, these
elements from the pretexts and combination of happenings
which had to be contrived so that the play might exist. The
plot, the intrigue, the incidents soon fade, and whatever
interest may have attached to the dramatic apparatus as
such vanishes. It was merely a crime: wished-for incest,
murder committed by proxy, with of course a god to carry
out the act. But what can be made of a crime once the
horror of it has subsided, once justice has been done, and
death has claimed the innocent and the guilty alike, for death
like the sea closes over every temporary scheme of events
and acts. The emotion born of the presence and condensation
of the drama disappears along with the decor, while the
gripped heart and eyes, which had so long remained fixed,
find relief from the constraint exerted upon the whole being
by the speaking, luminous stage.

Everyone disappears, save the queen: poor, pitiable

Hippolyte, the moment he lies shattered on the resounding shore; Théramène, his message just declaimed; Thésée, Aricie, Œnone, and Invisible Neptune himself—all melt into absence. They have stopped pretending to be, having *been* only to serve the author's essential design. They were not made of lasting substance; their roles have used them up. They live only long enough to incite the ardor and wrath, the remorse and terrors typical of a woman *insane* with desire; they are used to bring forth from her Racinian depths the noblest expressions of concupiscence and remorse ever inspired by passion. They do not survive, but she does. Memory reduces the work to a monologue; within me it changes from its originally dramatic form into a purely lyric one—for lyricism is precisely that, the transfiguration of a monologue.

Love, provoked beyond measure in the person of Phèdre, has none of the tenderness it assumes in Bérénice. She is ruled by the flesh whose sovereign voice calls, unanswerably, for the possession of the beloved's body and has one single goal: the perfect attunement of concordant ecstasies. Life thus falls prey to images so intense that its days and nights, its duties and its falsehoods are torn apart. The power of physical passion, forever thirsting because it is never slaked, may be compared to an open wound which keeps aggravating itself: it is an inexhaustible source of pain, for the pain can only increase while the wound remains open. That is its law. By definition, one cannot get used to it for it insists on its hideous presence as though it were always new. It is the same with an incurable love lodged in its victim.

With Phèdre, nothing veils, mitigates, ennobles, adorns, or

elevates her sexual frenzy. The mind, with its profound, subtle, shifting play, its outlets, its intuitions, its inquisitiveness, its refinements, can do nothing to embellish this consummately simple passion or divert it from itself. Phèdre has read nothing. Hippolyte is, for all we know, a fool. What does that matter? This incandescent queen needs only enough mind to serve her vengeance, invent stratagems, and enslave itself to instinct. As for the soul, it becomes nothing more than its obsessive power, the ruthless and unwavering will to clasp its prey, draw him under, to moan and die of pleasure at his side.

This love, devoid of metaphysics, is love as described or presupposed in the literature of an age which rarely mentioned the soul except in philosophical speculations, an age when lovers were never seen invoking the universe between embraces and fretting over "the World as Will and Idea" by their bedside.

True, gods in that day loved no more deeply than men. Moreover, they took an interest in our endeavors, furthering them, foiling them, even mixing in them just like ordinary mortals except that they were more powerful, no broader in mind but smaller in heart, with fewer scruples to thwart their instincts, to oppose their caprices, nothing to temper their perversions, their ardor, and made of such incorruptible stuff that they could burn with desire yet not be consumed by it. On occasion these sublime lovers would fertilize our females, an uncanny phenomenon posing a problem of metabiology quite like the one we find in a remarkable verse of Genesis, which has prompted more than one solution.

Racine knew better than to sweeten that desire in the

raw which Phèdre radiates and sings. She could scarcely have inherited from her makers, Minos and Pasiphaë, what was not in their nature. It was not given them to feel as we do, when we yield unreservedly to the weakness of cherishing another person, a surge of tenderness that deliciously calms and eases all the forces of the soul. They were a callous pair of beings. Primitive love, as it appears in most myths, shows nothing but its implacably instinctive essence. It is, at this stage, simply a "force of nature," borne and acknowledged as such. It does not yearn for the exaltation that comes of One and One uniting beyond, through, above their keenest mutual spasm: it is satisfied to be this visceral lurch, for nature requires nothing more enduring than a flash. In simple love, anything that distracts from the consummation of pleasure runs contrary to nature. This necessary and sufficient love is too intent on seizing the body of its prey to spare its sensibilities; it will get what it wants by hook or by crook. It is not at all above fraud, rape, abduction. The gods of that age, whose sole function it was to enact the designs vainly suggested to us by our desire, accomplish effortlessly what we can only dream of doing: they make sport of feelings as well as of natural laws and, by force, by guile, or even by corrupting if need be, they satisfy their cravings. Mythology is essentially bestial. Zeus turns into a swan, an eagle, a bull, a shower of gold, a cloud, thus refusing to take advantage of his identity. The conquest itself is all that matters to him: he does not care to figure in dreams. But perhaps these metamorphoses are only symbols of the various tricks and ploys men use to achieve their sensual goals, replying, as the occasion and their wits dictate, on one advantage or another, on a repertory of grimaces, exploiting their visible manliness, their fortune, their fame, their brilliance—or the opposite of all these, for there are unfortunates whose misfortune, whose ugliness, even to deformity, will excite a feeling of pity verging on love, and move some heart to give its all; nothing is impossible where human taste is concerned, and I have observed the oddest conquests.

Though his Phèdre is largely ruled by instinct, Racine presents her feral nature in the most elegant terms, revealing its depths as the drama unfolds. The particular case that his tragedy lays bare would, moreover, appear to be less anomalous than deplorable. Unrequited love cries for vengeance. God Himself says to us, "Love me, love me or I shall deal you eternal death." And in the Bible we read that "Joseph, being well-made and comely, it came to pass that the wife of his master cast her eyes upon him, and said, 'Lie with me.'" Courteously rebuffed, Potiphar's wife denounced him, charging him with seeking to take her by force, just as Thésée's wife accused Hippolyte and so brought down upon him the paternal curse, executed by Neptune. I fear, then, that in our mind's eye we must see Phèdre in the same pitiless light as Rembrandt saw Potiphar's wife. In his engraving he showed her furiously twisting and stretching toward Joseph, who is straining to get away. The etching is remarkable for its powerful lewdness. In it, the biblical female, her belly naked, fleshy, dazzling white, exposed, clings to Joseph's robe, while he strives to tear himself from the clutches of this stark madwoman whose transport drags not only her ponderous flesh, but the whole soft bulk of her devastated bed, spilling a tangle of sheets to the floor. Everything focuses on this delirious belly, which sustains, concentrates, and radiates the painting's luminous power.

Never has desire unleashed been portrayed so brutally, with a keener sense of the ignoble force that compels flesh to offer itself like the yawning of a monster's jaws. The Egyptian woman is not beautiful, but there is no reason why she need be. Through her plainness she shows how confident she is that her aroused and desperate sex will prevail unaided. This is not an uncommon error; it is not always an error. Yet I cannot imagine Phèdre otherwise than very beautiful, in the full flower of beauty, of her beauty, which I shall come to presently.

The passion of love secretes a fatal poison that is, at first, only faintly active, easily eliminated, and passes unnoticed. But a few trifles can quicken it so that, suddenly, it can overwhelm all our powers of reason, and our fear of men and gods.

By this I mean that, in becoming strongly enamored of someone, we unconsciously invest the object of our love with a power to make us suffer which far surpasses the power we grant him or her (and look for) to make us rapturously happy. And if the need to possess some one person takes such complete hold of us as to form the condition of life itself (which is the way absolute love works), this now-vital affection, once it is torn by despair, sets little store by life. It familiarly entertains the idea of murder. This soon mingles with the idea of suicide; which is absurd, thus natural.

Having lost hope, Phèdre kills. Having killed, she kills herself.

Phèdre cannot be a very young woman. She is at the age when women who are truly, one might even say expressly, born for love, come into possession of their powers. She has reached that moment when life recognizes its fullness and its unfulfillment. In the offing are physical decay, rebuffs, and her own ashes. But here and now, bursting with life, she can experience feeling to its uttermost degree. What she is worth dictates, in the recesses of her mind, what she desires, so that her burdensome resources very gradually devote themselves to some potential but unknown plunderer who will take them by surprise, exalt and then exhaust them; whoever he is, for he has not even appeared yet, he is already gifted with all the charms conferred on him by impatient suspense, by a thirst every moment more searing. The internal processes of our living substance lose their normal function, which is to assure the survival of the organism. The body comes to anticipate the self, and to see farther ahead. It floods with a superabundant sense of being, and the mysterious anxiety arising from this excess riots in dreams, in temptations, in risks, in feverish attention alternating with lapses of mind. The flesh itself becomes a proposal. Like a plant overwhelmed by the weight of its own fruit, and bent forward as though begging to be plucked, woman offers herself.

Perhaps this has to do with some dark conflict being waged between the forces that so strangely coexist in our beings—and ones which continually produce us, that is, which keep us living, and the others which tend only to reproduce us. The individual succumbs to the species, which insidiously promotes itself throughout the whole person whose sensibility and general economy are invaded by the energies of a minute egg as it ripens, becoming at once the product, the disturbing component, the enemy, and finally dominating the whole living body. The injunction to outlive struggles and pits itself against the importance of living. The indefinable sensations provoked by an unmated seed influence, *by remote control*, the whole mental disposition, which has been so primed for the coming adventure that it will see in it, when it does unfold, an event of infinite magnitude. *Venus* calls the tune and *Psyche* plays.

Phèdre is in the midst of her second puberty, and embodies all the alienation, the anxiety of that age.

What I have said up to now was by way of preparation for that eminently noteworthy adjective set in the famous line:

C'est Vénus tout entière. . . .

So Venus is the culprit, and Venus "tout entière." How can this name Venus be translated into nonallegorical language, and what is the precise meaning of "tout entière," an expression so admirable and felicitous that I hesitate to belabor it? Racine could take such perfection in his stride, without lingering over it, but today these words have connotations which his age did not as yet clearly recognize. We are able to uncover treasures the author did not suspect he had buried and see in his words evidence of a prescient mind. This prescience refers to the physiological aspect which, for lack of knowledge, I shall not explore, but I believe I have suggested the lines that someone more expert might follow, and I shall confine myself to what little I can say, offhand.

With Phèdre having come to the unstable pass I have described, her life has all the makings of an emotional tempest. Suddenly the event takes place. Someone appears and is at once recognized as the very one who was destined to appear.

Why not someone else? We are always free to wonder
if any other captain of handsome presence might have
brought matters to a head. But no, it was Hippolyte, who
draws down upon himself the burden of desire that weighed
so heavily on her uneasy soul. Instantly, everything is
transformed, within her—and around her. The days change
color. Even the passage of time becomes irregular. The
body's organic routines are upset. The heart is caught, and
the breath as well: a glance, a hesitation, a hint, a footfall,
a shadow will quicken or suspend them. The basic functions
of life have found their master... in a phantom, in a trou-
bling figment. Incredible superstitions gain credence. Her
mind has astonishing lapses, or pays obsessed attention; it
gives birth to the maddest inventions, or falls into a stupor
lasting for hours, for days during which it shows no palp-
able signs of thought, as if it were arrested, like the body of a
wounded man who expects intolerable pain to come of his
least movement. All those vain ornaments, those veils,
would not seem so heavy to the queen were she not a woman
already overwhelmed by love. Her entire life is reorganized
around a fundamental anxiety, all values are at the mercy of
a whim that is not hers, subordinated to the infinite Value
she attaches to Another, to the promise he seemed to embody.
And when, having offered him her entire being (a gesture
that in itself compromises her organic, psychic, and social
equilibrium), this all-embracing gift is answered with resist-
ance and refusal, then all the honey of prospective ecstasies,
all the sap of hoped-for love, whose influence had over-
charged her inmost vitality, all this turns into a poison of
the rarest virulence. There is nothing which that distillation
of hatred and fury does not attack, corrode, and eat away.
The vital exchanges, the natural functions, the habits, the

ethical and civil laws that firmly establish a person within his life, fall apart. *C'est Vénus tout entière à sa proie attachée.* When Venus first grew fast to her, the woman in love appeared transfigured by a relish for life, by a will to ascend the highest heights of ecstasy, her desire exerting such influence that her very flesh grew increasingly desirable as her desire grew increasingly ardent. Phèdre, beautiful in her own right but, like all beautiful women, beautiful even before love, attains the full splendor of her beauty when she declares her passion. I say *splendor* because the fire of a decisive act illumines her face, makes her eyes glow and animates her entire person. But afterward, that sublime brow falters; it is overwhelmed by pathos; it sags beneath its burden, and the eyes grow dim. Pain, the lesion of the soul, contrives a new and frightful beauty—a mask whose pinched features alter to those of a Fury. Venus is at last abandoning her prey. The venom of love has done its work. A woman has passed through the successive stages of passion; there is nothing left for her to do on earth. One draught of a different poison, the product of ordinary chemistry, will spirit her to Hades for a final reckoning.

As for the language of this play, I shall not importune the reader by saying the obvious, or what has been said before, very often and very well. I shall not sing the praises of a form that achieves the consummate synthesis of art and the natural, that carries its prosodic chains so lightly as to make of them an ornament, a kind of garment draping the nakedness of thought. In *Phèdre*, the strict discipline of our Alexandrine retains and fosters a higher form of freedom; it makes eloquence sound so easy that one does not at first realize what craft and labors of transmutation that ease must have entailed. I shall take the liberty of relating an experience I had once, for in my mind it is inseparably bound to what I have just written. I hope that this personal anecdote will not be seen as an intrusion of vanity. Not many years ago, I composed the libretto of a cantata, and had to do it rather quickly, in Alexandrines. One day, I laid this work aside to go to the Academy and, my mind still absorbed in working out the cadence of a period, I found myself gazing absent-mindedly through a shopwindow on the quai, where a lovely page of verse stood on display, beautifully printed in large typeface. A remarkable interchange sprang up between myself and this fragment of noble architecture. As though still at work on my draft, unconsciously, for the better part of a minute I began to try out word conversions on the exhibited text. I felt like a sculptor who had seized a chunk of marble, while dreaming that he was molding soft and still moist clay.

But the text would not allow itself to be rehandled. *Phèdre* resisted me. I thus learned, through direct experience and immediate sensation, what is meant by perfection in a work. It was a rude awakening.

At The Lamoureux Concert in 1893

AM I REALLY permitted to speak here—disarranging the music stands, irrupting in the midst of the marvelous strings, the suave woodwinds, the all-powerful brass, not as a singer, but simply to make myself heard in a voice neither tuneful nor harmonious, and with no guidance from M. Wolff's baton? I confess it moves me deeply to find myself, alone of my kind, in this essentially enchanted forest, whose ramifications of sound can respond with such tenderness or violence to the breath of genius.

How am I to justify being made to break the spell in this way? I feel as ashamed and guilty as the man who, arriving during the performance of some orchestral work at the old Cirque d'Été, would see Lamoureux give a short, terrifying tap with his baton, stopping the performance, to turn slowly round towards him, arms folded, and confound the intruder with a sudden, absolute, thunderous silence. A thousand concentrated glares would reduce him to ashes.

What explanation can there be for this sacrilege, this intrusion of a writer, of a writer's flat and toneless speech into the holy of holies?

It is simply because literature owes a tremendous debt to Charles Lamoureux, a debt to be repaid as best it may be.

First it must be remarked that any history of literature at the end of the nineteenth century which made no mention of music would be futile; worse than incomplete, it would be inaccurate; worse than inaccurate, unintelligible. Besides, any literary history, in general, which confined itself to literature would be as unreliable as would be, for example, a political history that omitted all mention of economic events.

Every period has its own great excitements, its grand topics of the moment, and these always mark its literature, though sometimes indirectly.

Let me say at once that the poetic movement which has developed from 1840 or '50 to the present day can in no way be understood, unless the profoundly important part played by music in that remarkable transformation is emphasized, elucidated, and given some definition. The musical education of the French public—and of an increasing number of French writers in particular—did more than any theoretic consideration to give poetry a purer sense of itself, and eliminate from its work whatever can be exactly expressed in prose. Just as music, from the beginning, sorted out what the ear receives—rejecting *noises*, which have their own kind of meaning but cannot be satisfactorily combined, in favor of musical *sounds*, which have no meaning in themselves but which can be readily reproduced and composed—in the same way poetry has done its utmost, not without some effort and risk, to choose from language those expressions in which sense, rhythm, sonority, and movement strengthen and harmonize with each other, at the same time trying to banish all expressions in which the sense is independent of musical form, of any auditory value.

In the period between 1880 and 1900, Lamoureux and the Lamoureux Concerts were capital influences in this re-education of poetry. What the Lamoureux Concerts were to Mallarmé and his followers, the Pasdeloup Concerts had been to Baudelaire.

Charles Lamoureux was the soul of scrupulousness, zea strictness, and honor in his admirable calling—a truly sacre calling, for the musical conductor must combine the qual ties of critic and votary, connoisseur and enchanter, lead and virtuoso. A strange soloist is the conductor, a multip performer compounded of a hundred and twenty execu tants. Maestro, you are none other than a Fabulous Monste

The nobility of Lamoureux' nature, his very fastidiou ness, his perfectionism and passion for detail were we suited to the almost religiously aesthetic period throug which we lived as young men.

The youth of the time saw in art the only outlet, the onl possible remaining field of development for its highe feelings. The artistic act, the emotion conveyed by works art seemed the only objects unquestionably worth our lov our labor, our longing, the only way to redemption; the were, in short, the only graspable certainties, safe beyond a the attacks of criticism, able to inspire all the force of fait without requiring any belief.

It was music—and orchestral music in particular—tha proved to be the one among all the arts most capable instilling, and even aggravating, such feelings of certaint and power.

Moreover, in the hierarchy of the arts, music on th grand scale as created by modern masters provides a re parallel with the powerful, the almost superabundan resources which other moderns have been able to create i the realm of material enterprise. In a way, this large-sca music can draw upon almost unlimited reserves of aestheti power. It plays with life's depths, the extremes of passio simulates the complexities of thought, and seems to st nature itself; rousing, soothing, exploring the whole nervo

stem—and all this by an almost instantaneous and irresist-
le agency, sometimes with a single note. Music plays upon
s, saddening, enlivening, intoxicating, rendering us thought-
l, at its own will making us more passionate or profound,
nderer or stronger than man ever was before.

Just as our machines can perform our labors for us, giving
s the benefit of speeds which far exceed our natural capacity,
music on the grand scale—with its ecstasies and rages
ways in wait to seize on us, its limitless imaginings, its
most total powers of possession—offers and inspires us
ith states of feeling that are half unreal yet more powerful
an most of our real ones. Not one of the other arts can
aim such sovereignty.

It is consequently not surprising if this music took on the
ature of a cult. It preached the cause of art, and at the same
me, as an experience in itself, it penetrated the whole
ffective and psychic being—and more than this, it was
trinsically one of the highest pleasures.

It was at once an intense stimulus to inner experience
nd a form of communion. A thousand people gathered
gether, inspired by the same cause to close their eyes and
ndergo the same intense emotion, can each feel absolutely
one and yet identified by this inner feeling with all their
eighbors who have thus become truly *one* with them—this
rms the ideal religious state, the oneness in feeling of a
ving multitude.

Music can produce artificially what otherwise results
om great public joys and sorrows, on the solemn days when
eople who do not know each other converse in the streets
nd might quite easily embrace.

This cult, then, this sacred function, this rite is what we
elebrated at the Cirque d'Été in my young days. From the

end of autumn until the end of spring, the Lamoureux Concert was the weekly event that sanctified the aesthetic faithful, and in particular the poets.

Picture to yourself that vanished arena, gorged to overflowing with all Paris could offer as its most elegant, its profoundest, its most inspired participants—a gathering from which there rose a heat as stifling as it was stimulating.

Lamoureux would appear; always dignified; never smiling, even in answer to applause. He would mount the podium, as if he were ascending to the altar, to sovereign authority; which is in fact what he was doing. He was about to promulgate the divine laws of Music.

He would raise his arms...and with that gesture hold six hundred souls in suspense. At once hearts would begin to beat and sigh in unison. Devout concentration, and a thrilling responsiveness would set in. No one dared to think of making the slightest movement, for in the rotunda of the Cirque there were two totally and almost brutally intolerant entities: one was Lamoureux; the other was ourselves, the young people who piled into the two-franc seats in the galleries—fanatics all, and ready, like all purists, to massacre whoever was so base as to let his chair squeak, or to give audible signs of a cold.

But on a bench in the Promenade, shaded and concealed by a wall of standing men, there sat one strange listener who, by supreme favor, enjoyed free entry to the Cirque: it was STÉPHANE MALLARMÉ, listening with rapture—and with that angelic sense of affliction provoked by the loftiest rivalries—to the enchantments of Beethoven or Wagner. As a great artist of language, his mind would be full of protest, and of a striving to decipher what the gods of pure sound could utter

NOTES

NOTES

vi. INSCRIPTIONS FOR THE PALAIS DE CHAILLOT: Four inscriptions composed for the new Palais de Chaillot, built for the International Exposition of 1937. It replaced the Palais du Trocadéro. The inscriptions, first published in *Les Nouvelles littéraires* (Paris, July 7, 1937), were criticized and even ridiculed in the press for their "obscurity" and "pretentiousness." Translated by Roger Shattuck.

In *Le Libertaire* (Paris, September 16, 1937), the following bit of spoofing appeared under the signature of "Monsieur Dubalai" (Mr. Newbroom):

Stung to emulation, one of the doorkeepers at the Trocadéro Museum has taken upon himself to remodel the inscriptions affixed over the entrances, while keeping to the Valerian form. Here is the result:

> *Francs par entrée, nombre cinq.*
> *Demi seulement pour militaires.*
> *De la guerre, mutilés et veuves,*
> *Gratuitement céans pénètrent.*

> (Francs for admittance, five in number.
> Half-price, only in uniform.
> The wounded or widowed in war
> Without fee may pervade herein.)

Confronted by this outburst of humbuggery, the public remains petrified, and their purses as obstinately concealed as the content of the Valerian lines.

Valéry replied to his critics in a "Note to the Reader," published in a deluxe edition of *Les Quatre Inscriptions du Palais de Chaillot* (with "Genèse du Papier," by Maurice Deléon, a frontispiece by Aristide Maillol, and printed in eighty copies on a handpress by the master printer, Raphael Maillol), Paris, 1938:

On a certain day in the year MCMXXXVII, there came to me a letter from the Eminent Architects of the new Palais du Trocadéro, known to some as the Palais de Chaillot.

The tenor of their request was that I compose Four Inscriptions, intended for four pediments on the building then in course of completion: each to be arranged in five lines, of about thirty-five signs or letters to a line. The lettering, in metal coated with gold leaf and forty centimeters high, would be affixed by bronze tenons to the stone at a height of twenty-five yards.

I was amazed by this order, and my first impulse was to decline. What could be said in a voice pitched so high? And in words meant to withstand the sun, and millions of eyes?

I have a certain imp of the arduous in me, and he took to the idea. Then again I have a taste for brevity, a taste rather stimulated by this challenge, even though it deplored the necessity, the enormity of *five* lines. A one-line inscription would have been much more exciting.

In the end I said yes, in the spirit of taking on a bet or a challenge; and I set about my problem of four unknown quantities. It led to a number of considerations, this sort of thing being new to me. I had at one time or another mused over mottos for sundials: there are some fine ones, a few profoundly memorable. But in the present case, the occasion and the terms were official, formidable, calculated to paralyze the pen. To write above men's height is a dizzying project: to write something one knows will remain forever public, staring down the endless variety of people who pass, surviving oneself; growing awkward or obscure, absurd or meaningless, alien, to the gazes that rise according to chance, mood, or a trick of the light. . . .

And what can be inscribed on monuments not designed to commemorate some particular great deed, or to blazon the glory of an individual? The Pantheon is there to receive illustrious ashes. On the Carrousel Arch, above the rose-red marble pilasters, a splendid phrase is engraved:

> AT THE EMPEROR NAPOLEON'S WORD
> FELL THE GERMAN EMPIRE. . . .

But here there was no dedicatee. Then I had the—sufficiently ancient and classical—notion of making these halls speak for themselves: let them say what they are and avow their ideals. As Museums, they collect the beautiful and rare; but the finest and rarest object is a dead thing unless the living eye gives it life. So it was to this I made my inscriptions give utterance.

There was no dearth of critics. Their absence would have been a sinister omen. Paris would not be Paris if these unlikely screeds had met with everyone's satisfaction. If anyone else had composed them, I have no doubt I would have made fun of them in my own way. Nevertheless I have a complaint. I am in no way shocked by blame or ridicule—every undertaking is their rightful prey. But if a man has claims to be a writer, then honor requires him to show his courage by offering the solution he would himself have found for the four inscriptions. If the passerby mocks or condemns, what more natural: he is only a judge. But the writer is always more or less involved in the issue. And if he does me damage he is implying "I could do better!", without saying what. . . .

I will end by offering to anyone interested a fifth inscription, which a museum might put over its entry to turn away the idle and the merely chilly:

> N'entre pas pour trouver ici
> Un abri contre l'eau du ciel:
> La pluie est bonne pour celui
> D'esprit stérile et de cœur sec.

221

(Do not enter here to find
A shelter from a watery sky:
Rain is excellent for him
Whose heart is dry and mind barren.)
(Translated by David Paul)

Introduction by Roger Shattuck

xi. *Valéry's poetic production was confined to two brief periods...*: Scholars now working on Valéry's personal papers and unpublished manuscripts have discovered evidence of a new poetic output toward the end of his life. (R.S.)

xiii. *"to amuse myself by translating..."*: *Cahiers* 1: 116.

xvi. *"Action is a fleeting madness...."*: See *Œuvres II*, Pléiade (1960), p. 612.

xviii. *on art not as embodying eternal and autonomous aesthetic value...*: The "art" housed in the Musée de l'Homme (the north wing of the Palais de Chaillot) is ethnographic and anthropological in nature: masks, idols, clothing, ornaments, utensils, weapons, etc. Such objects are produced in the daily life of human beings in society, and all such objects "express" and refer to a set of acts or gestures, like hunting and worship, of which they are a part. Thus in speaking of art in this context, Valéry is closer to the *craft* tradition than to that of fine arts. (R.S.)

xxiii. *We cannot be everything at once.* I believe that Proust is describing the same profound instability or vibratory character of the psyche when he speaks of "les intermittences du cœur." It is revealing that Jacques Rivière used Proust's expression in referring to borderline mental states in his correspondence with Antonin Artaud. The clinical label, schizophrenia, clearly is inappropriate to describe such a state of being known to us all. (R.S.)

The Aesthetic Infinite: "L'Infini esthétique," *Œuvres II*, Pléiade (1960), p. 1342. See Collected Works, vol. 13.

xxv. *"Civilization sustains itself..."*: *Cahiers* 2: 738.

xxvi. *" The doing means more to me..."*: *Œuvres I*, Pléiade (1960), pp. 51–52.

xxvii. *the twenty-nine monumental volumes of his notebooks...*: In 1922, just as he was entering "public life," Valéry wrote to Gide from London: "Anyway, I always have to come back to the question of my famous notes. I may end up deliberately believing I did nothing till I was forty-five. Still, the real me is there in the notes" (*Œuvres II*, Pléiade (1960), p. 1490). From 1894 on, Valéry wrote daily in his *Cahiers*. We may owe both their existence and their unsystematic form to his long study of Leonardo da Vinci, which began the same year. A sampling of the 28,000 pages indicates that they contain little poetry, very few first drafts of published prose texts, and only indirect, uncircumstantial accounts of his daily life or of encounters and conversations with people, etc. Mathematical symbols occur frequently in carefully worked problems. There are occasional ink drawings. In the twentieth century, Whitehead's and Wittgenstein's writings best bear comparison with Valéry's for range and depth. Those three minds moved along intersecting lines of tension that connect language and mathematics. The similarities in form and style between Valéry and Wittgenstein are particularly striking. (The Centre National de la Recherche Scientifique published the

Cahiers in 1958, apparently with some materials omitted.) (R.S.)

"*ne pas écrire à la suite*"; "*Literature growing wild*": *Œuvres II*, Pléiade (1960), p. 1483.

The Art of Poetry: see Collected Works, Vol. 7.

xxix. See my essay "The Tortoise and the Hare: a Study of Valéry, Freud, and Leonardo da Vinci," in *The Origins of Modern Consciousness*, ed. John Weiss (Detroit, 1965), and in *Leonardo da Vinci: Aspects of the Renaissance Genius*, ed. Morris Philipson (New York, 1966). (R.S.)

3. RECEPTION ADDRESS TO THE FRENCH ACADEMY: "Discours prononcés dans la séance publique tenue par l'Académie Française pour la réception de M. Paul Valéry, le jeudi 23 juin, 1927," Paris, Typographie de Firmin-Didot, Imprimeurs de l'Institut de France, 1927; published with the "Réponse" by Gabriel Hanotaux. Valéry's address first appeared in the newspapers *Les Débats* and *Le Temps*, June 24, 1927; it was published as a "plaquette" with the title *Discours de réception à l'Académie Française*, in *Œuvres: Discours*, Volume E, Paris, N.R.F., 1935, and in *Variété IV* (1938): see *Œuvres I*, Pléiade (1957), p. 714. Translated here by Frederick Brown.

4. *René Boylesve*: a novelist elected to the Academy in 1918; he died in 1926. His novel *Tu n'es plus rien* (1917) is a study of the changes in feeling and opinion which resulted from the first World War.

6. *One garret even gained renown...*: a reference to the Académie des Goncourts, a literary society founded by Edmond de Goncourt (1822–96), who willed his estate for its endowment. The idea of an academy had grown out of the group of friends and disciples who gathered on Sundays

in the "garret" of the Goncourts' house in Auteuil. Each year, the Goncourt Academy gives a prize to the author of the best published prose work of the year.

12. *the very man needed...*: this phrase is the first of a series of indirect references to Anatole France, whose chair Valéry was taking in the Academy. On this occasion, when Valéry was expected to eulogize France, he refused to speak his name, choosing to identify him only as "the man who took his country's name for his own." This startling outrage was Valéry's revenge, no doubt, for Anatole France's sorry opinion of Mallarmé.

Henri Mondor, in his *Mallarmé: Documents iconographiques* (Geneva, 1947), gives the following account: Banville, Coppée, and France were chosen by a publisher to supervise the selection of poems for the third *Parnasse contemporain*, an anthology. France proved to be an unyielding and acrimonious critic of Verlaine and Mallarmé. In refusing their poems, he said of Verlaine: "No, this author does not deserve to be included; his verse is the worst I ever read." Speaking of Mallarmé, "whose *Hérodiade* had been the glory of the previous *Parnasse contemporain*, and whose *Afternoon of a Faun* was to become one of the most admired masterpieces in all of lyric poetry, France made a cowardly response: 'We would be laughed at,' he said."

15. *they die first as men, then as great men*: When Anatole France died in 1924, the Surrealists seized the opportunity to publicize themselves by issuing a virulent obituary entitled *Un Cadavre*, in which they figuratively spat on his grave. André Breton summarized their feelings in the following peroration:

Let us mark with a beautiful, white asterisk this year 1924 which has put to rest three shifty customers—Loti, Barrès, and France: the

idiot, the traitor, and the cop. With Anatole France a bit of human
servility has passed away. A holiday should be declared to celebrate
the burial of chicanery, traditionalism, patriotism, opportunism,
skepticism, and poverty of heart! Let us bear in mind that France
served as godfather to the most infamous ham actors of this era and
let us never forgive him, with his smiling inertia, for having flown
the colors of revolution at half-mast. We would do well to empty a
bookstall on the quais of the old books "he loved so well," place
his corpse in it, and hurl the whole thing into the Seine.

17. *Jules Vallès*: (1832–85), novelist and radical journalist,
author of *Jacques Vingtras*, an autobiographical novel in
three parts: *L'Enfant, Le Bachelier, L'Insurgé*.

Petit Chose: *Le Petit Chose* (1868) is a semi-autobio-
graphical novel by Alphonse Daudet.

Jean Servien: the hero of Anatole France's novel *Les
Désirs de Jean Servien* (1882).

19. *an imperious presence...*: France's mistress, Mme.
Arman de Caillavet, prevailed upon him to spend long hours
writing in an upstairs study, in her mansion on the Avenue
de la Reine-Hortense (now Avenue Hoche). Her salon,
where Anatole France reigned, also included Jules Lemaître
and Marcel Proust. She died in 1910.

25. *oracular reeds*: "roseaux parlants," recalls the passage
from Pascal's *Pensées*, Pléiade, III, 264: "L'homme n'est
qu'un roseau, le plus faible de la nature; mais c'est un roseau
pensant." ("Man is only a reed, the weakest in all of nature;
but he is a thinking reed.")

27. *A single incident might explode....*: Valéry is probably
thinking of the Dreyfus affair. Anatole France, along with
Zola, had defended Dreyfus.

32. *Joseph de Maistre*: (1753–1821), Valéry greatly admired
this reactionary political philosopher, diplomat, and historian.

Maistre spent fourteen years as ambassador in St. Petersburg; a fiery critic of the French Revolution, his faith was in God, the Pope, and the King; see his *Les Soirées de Saint-Pétersbourg* (1821). (See Collected Works, Vol. 10, pp. 165–66 and *n*; and Vol. 13, p. 54 and *n*.)

38. IN HONOR OF ÉMILE VERHAEREN: "A speech inaugurating the monument to Émile Verhaeren, in the garden of the church of Saint-Séverin, in Paris, November 10, 1927," Paris, Firmin-Didot, Imprimeurs de l'Institut de France, 1927. Published under the title "Discours sur Verhaeren" with other speeches in a supplement to the *Bulletin Municipal officiel*, Wednesday, December 21, 1927; same title, Champion, Paris, 1927; in *Œuvres: Discours*, Vol. E, Paris, *N.R.F.*, 1935; see *Œuvres I*: Pléiade (1957), p. 756.

Verhaeren was the principal Belgian poet of the late nineteenth and early twentieth centuries. Born at St.- Amand, near Antwerp, in 1855, he died beneath the wheels of a train at Rouen in 1916. (Translated here by Frederick Brown.)

Henry Carton de Wiart: (1869–1951), Belgian statesman and professor of sociology; he also wrote novels and stories and was active in Catholic social propaganda among workers.

40. *Jean Moréas*: pseudonym of Iannis Papadiamantopoulos (1856–1910), a Greek born in Athens, who moved to Paris and became a leading French poet of the late nineteenth century.

41. *Georges Rodenbach*: (1855–98), a leading Belgian poet of the last half of the nineteenth century; he grew up in Bruges and is perhaps best known for his novel *Bruges-la morte* (1892). He spent the last ten years of his life in Paris where he died.

41. *Maurice Maeterlinck*: (1862–1949). Born in Ghent, in 1886 he went to Paris and allied himself with the young Symbolist poets. His early poems *Serres chaudes* and *La Princesse Maleine* (1889) made him famous; his plays *L'Intruse* and *Les Aveugles* (1890), *Pelléas et Mélisande* (1892), and *Intérieur* (1892) established his reputation. He was awarded the Nobel Prize in literature in 1911; he lectured in the United States in 1920, and returned in 1940, a refugee from the second World War.

Ruysbroeck the Admirable: (1293–1381), the Blessed Jan van Ruysbroeck, called "the Admirable," a medieval mystic born at Ruysbroeck, near Brussels. He died at the monastery of Groenendael, near Waterloo, where he had withdrawn with several companions to meditate and write. Among his contemporaries, Geert Groote, Tauler, and Thomas a Kempis considered Ruysbroeck their master.

47. REPLY TO MARSHAL PÉTAIN'S RECEPTION ADDRESS TO THE FRENCH ACADEMY: Published with Pétain's address, "Discours prononcés dans la Séance Publique tenue par l'Académie Française pour la réception de M. le Maréchal Pétain, le jeudi 22 janvier 1931," Paris, Firmin-Didot, Imprimeurs de l'Institut de France, 1931. The speeches appeared the next day, January 23, 1931, in *Le Temps*, and were published as *Discours de Réception de M. le Maréchal Pétain à l'Académie Française et Réponse de M. Paul Valéry*, Paris, *N.R.F.* and Plon, 1931; in *Œuvres: Discours*, Vol. E, Gallimard, 1935; in *Variété IV*, Paris, 1938. See *Œuvres I*, Pléiade (1957), p. 1098. Translated by David Paul.

Philippe Pétain: (1856–1951), Marshal of France, was born at Cauchy-à-la-Tour (Pas de Calais). He served as head of the French state during the German occupation (1940–

45), and after the liberation was condemned to death (August 15, 1945). The sentence was commuted to life imprisonment on the Île d'Yeu.

59. *Throughout forty years Europe is held in suspense...*: In an essay written in 1897, "A Conquest by Method," Valéry had expressed his views on the threat of Germany to Europe. See Collected Works, Vol. 10.

79. *But perhaps we should never look to war—or even to political action—for the power to establish a genuine peace?*: as a member of the Permanent Committee on Arts and Letters of the Committee on Intellectual Co-operation of the League of Nations, Valéry was active in the Committee's effort to bring about a state of mutual understanding between peoples through intellectual co-operation. For his activities in the League of Nations, see Collected Works, Vol. 10.

80. *...the dearest disciple and warmest friend of Marshal Foch...*: a reference to Max Weygand, General of the French Army, born in Brussels (1867–1965); elected to the French Academy in 1931.

84. COMMENCEMENT ADDRESS TO THE LEGION OF HONOR'S SCHOOL FOR GIRLS AT SAINT-DENIS: "Discours prononcé à la distribution des prix de la Maison d'Éducation de la Légion d'Honneur de Saint-Denis, le 11 juillet 1932," Melun, Imprimerie Administrative, 1933; republished as "Discours à la Maison d'Éducation de la Légion d'Honneur," *Œuvres*: *Discours*, Vol. E, Paris, 1935; and in *Variété IV*, Paris, Gallimard, 1938. See *Œuvres I*, Pléiade (1957), p. 1419. Translated here by Roger Shattuck.

"La Maison d'Éducation de la Légion d'Honneur de Saint-Denis" was one of the schools instituted by Napoleon I in 1805 to educate the daughters of members of the Legion of Honor. It was established in 1809 in the buildings of the secularized Abbey of St. Denis, whose church had for centuries been the royal and mortuary basilica.

85. *two divertissements given at Saint-Cyr*: Louis XIV and Mme. de Maintenon, in 1685, founded a convent school at St. Cyr for the daughters of poor noblemen; Racine's *Esther* (1689) and *Athalie* (1691) were first performed there. The convent was suppressed during the French Revolution, and in 1808, the École de Saint-Cyr, the French equivalent of West Point or Sandhurst, was established in the buildings.

94. ON HENRI BREMOND: "Inauguration d'une Plaque Commémorative du Séjour de M. Henri Bremond, 16 rue Chanoinesse, le 9 juin 1934, Discours de M. Paul Valéry," Firmin-Didot, Imprimeurs de l'Institut de France, 1934; reprinted in *La Vie Catholique*, June 16, 1934. Published as "Discours sur Henri Bremond" in *Œuvres: Discours*, Vol. E, Paris, Gallimard, 1935. See *Œuvres I*, Pléiade (1957), p. 763. Translated here by Frederick Brown.

Henri Bremond: (1865–1933), priest, literary critic, and historian, born at Aix-en-Provence, and educated by the Jesuits, he was a member of that Order until 1904 when he joined the secular clergy and devoted himself entirely to writing. His most important work is *L'Histoire littéraire du sentiment religieux en France* (6 vols., 1916–24); he is also known for his *Prière et poésie* (Prayer and Poetry) (1925), and *La Poésie pure* (1927). The latter stirred a literary controversy in the 1920's, over the question of pure poetry. Bremond was elected to the French Academy in 1923.

99. *Mistral*: Frédéric Mistral (1830–1914), Provençal poet, one of the founders of the Félibrige (1854), an

association to promote the linguistic and literary renaissance of Provence.

Grammar of Assent: written by John Henry Cardinal Newman (1870).

101. *Arthur Mugnier*: a canon of the church of Sainte-Clothilde, much appreciated for his learning and wit in the intellectual salons of Paris. Canon Mugnier was in large part responsible for the religious conversion of J.-K. Huysmans. See Collected Works, Vol. 9, index, *s.v.*

Maurice Barrès: (1862–1923), one of the eminent French writers of his time—elected to the French Academy in 1906. His themes evolved from youthful meditations on the inner self (the *moi*) toward a preoccupation with "the general interest" as the formative influence on the individual.

Countess of Noailles: (1876–1933), Anna-Élisabeth, princesse Brancovan; by marriage, comtesse de Noailles; French poet and novelist of Romanian origins, she was awarded the Academy's Grand Prix de Littérature in 1921. Her literary salon attracted most of the important writers of her time.

102. REPORT ON THE MONTYON AWARDS FOR VIRTUE: "Rapport sur les Prix de Vertu, par Paul Valéry, Directeur de l'Académie," Paris, Firmin-Didot, Imprimeurs de l'Institut de France, 1934; read at the annual public session on Thursday, December 20, 1934; reprinted the following day, December 21, 1934, in *Le Temps* and *Le Journal des Débats*. Published under the title *État de la Vertu, Rapport à l'Académie française*, Paris, Typographie Léon Pichon, 1935; as "Rapport sur les Prix de Vertu," in *Œuvres: Discours*, Vol. E, Paris, 1935, and in *Variété IV*, 1938. See *Œuvres I*, Pléiade (1957), p. 936. Translated for this edition by Frederick Brown.

Valéry's satire on the Awards for Virtue was coolly received by his audience and in the press. Under the heading "Scandal in the Academy" (*Libres Propos*, December 25, 1934), one journalist wrote: "In an article worthy of the great writers of the eighteenth century, Paul Valéry not only abused the Academy as no one else ever dared under the Dome; he even taught his colleague, the Marshal [Pétain], a lesson in the free man's contempt for the military training of youth and the cult of the State. The fact that not a single leftist newspaper reprinted his words under the title 'Voltaire versus Pétain'—this alone justifies our question: 'Do we still know how to read?'"

103. *What a character was this magnificent Montyon*: J. B. Auget, Baron de Montyon (1733–1820), a philanthropist and economist, held several important offices of state, among them that of chancellor to "Monsieur" (the younger brother of the King of France). In his will, Montyon left an endowment to the French Academy establishing three prizes, one of them being the *Prix de Vertu*, to be awarded to a poor Frenchman for "the most virtuous act."

a bequest of money which we must award every year to Virtue: Valéry was not the first man of letters to have a low opinion of the Montyon Prize. Flaubert wrote in his *Intimate Notebook, 1840–1841:* "These are the truly stupid things: 1. literary criticism, whatever it may be, good or bad; 2. the Temperance Society; 3. the Montyon Prize; 4. a man who praises the human species—a donkey eulogizing long ears."

108. *Infernal Regions—of libraries . . .*: "les Enfers: ceux des bibliothèques"; that part of a library, not open to the public, where books of a licentious nature are kept.

110. *Crownings of the Queen of the May . . .*: "couronne-

ments de rosières." *La rosière* was the girl designated as the most virtuous, crowned with roses, and given a dowry or some other recompense. The custom is said to have originated with St. Médard, the fifth-century seigneur of Salency and bishop of Noyon, who provided twenty-five French pounds (*livres*) and a crown of roses.

120. *M. Ernest Renan created quite a reputation for Sirius. . . . He brought back from there a certain point of view. . . .*: In a letter of December 31, 1886, to his friend, the great chemist Berthelot, Renan wrote, "Quand on se place au point de vue du système solaire, nos révolutions ont à peine l'amplitude de mouvements d'atomes. Du point de vue de Sirius c'est moins encore. Du point de vue de l'infini ce n'est rien." (From the point of view of the solar system, our revolutions have scarcely the scope of an atom's movement. From the point of view of Sirius, even less. From the point of view of infinity, none at all.) See Renan, *Œuvres complètes*, Vol. II, p. 1037.

Ernest Renan (1823–92), author of *L'Histoire des origines du christianisme* (1863–83); *La Vie de Jésus* (1863); *L'Avenir de la science* (1890).

129. ADDRESS TO THE CONGRESS OF SURGEONS: "Discours aux Chirurgiens, prononcé à la Séance d'inauguration du Congrès français de chirurgie, le lundi 17 octobre, 1938," Paris, Congrès français de chirurgie, 1938, 47ème session, Félix Alcan. Published as *Discours aux Chirurgiens*, Paris, Gallimard, 1938; in *Variété V*, Paris, 1944. See *Œuvres I*, Pléiade (1957), p. 907.

The following note precedes the title page in the Gallimard edition of 1938: "This lecture was delivered on Monday, 17 October 1938, in the Amphitheater of the School of

Medicine in Paris, at the opening session of the Congress on Surgery, held under the presidency of M. Paul Valéry, Honorary President, assisted by Professor Léon Imbert, honorary Dean of the School of Medicine in Marseilles, President of the Congress, and by Professor Henri Mondor, Secretary General." Translated here by Roger Shattuck.

141. *The very name of your profession*...: Surgery (*chirurgie*) derives from the Greek *cheirourgia*, "work of the hand."

146. *your Secretary General*...: Henri Mondor (1885–1962), Professor of Surgery in the School of Medicine of the University of Paris, was the author of works on Pasteur and Dupuytren, an eighteenth-century French surgeon, as well as a number of literary figures: Verlaine, Alain, and Valéry. He is known primarily, however, for his long devotion to Mallarmé: collecting his letters, manuscripts, and every possible source of information about him. He published a number of studies on Mallarmé, the most important being his immense volume *Vie de Mallarmé* (1947). Mondor was elected in 1946 to Valéry's chair in the Academy.

151. THE FUTURE OF LITERATURE: "L'Avenir de la littérature," translated by Malcolm Cowley, and published (April 22, 1928) in the Sunday book section of the *New York Herald Tribune*. The French text is apparently lost.

158. THE CENTENARY OF PHOTOGRAPHY: "Centenaire de la Photographie à la Sorbonne le 7 janvier 1939, Discours de M. Paul Valéry, délégué de l'Académie Française," Paris, Firmin-Didot, Imprimeurs de l'Institut de France, 1939; reprinted in *Bulletin de la Société d'Encouragement pour l'Industrie nationale*, Paris, January–February 1939, Nos. 1

and 2; in *Bulletin de la Société Française de Photographie et de Cinématographie: Commémoration du Centenaire de l'Apparition de la Photographie dans le Monde*, Paris, 4th series, Vol. I, No. 3, March 1939; reprinted in *Vues*, Paris, La Table Ronde, 1948. Translated here by Frederick Brown.

160. *And then came Daguerre*: "Enfin Daguerre vint." Valéry had a habit of making parodies of famous phrases, such as Boileau's *Enfin Malherbe vint* (*Art Poétique*, I).

168. A PERSONAL VIEW OF SCIENCE: "Vues personnelles sur la science," in *Patrie, Revue mensuelle illustré de l'Empire*, Algiers, No. 6, 1942 (first year); reprinted in *Vues*, Paris, La Table Ronde, 1948. Translated here by Roger Shattuck

180. MY THEATERS: "Mes Théâtres," in *Les Dernières Nouvelles* (newspaper), Algiers, September 19, 1942; reprinted in the review *La Nef*, May 1945; and in a volume of Valéry's miscellaneous writings, *Vues*, Paris, 1948. See *Œuvres I,* Pléiade (1957), p. 1791. Translated here by Frederick Brown.

184. *when I collaborated with Honegger...* : for accounts of this collaboration by both men, see Collected Works, Vol. 3, p. 220 and *n*.

185. ON PHÈDRE AS A WOMAN: "Sur Phèdre Femme," first published as "Prélude" to a monumental edition of *Phèdre, Tragédie de Racine*, Les Bibliophiles Franco-Suisse, illustrated with etchings by Richard Brunck de Freundeck, Paris, 1942; reprinted in *Variété V*, Paris, 1944. See *Œuvres I*, Pléiade (1957), p. 499. Translated here by Frederick Brown.

Julien P. Monod's copy of the edition, now in the *Valeryanum* of the Bibliothèque Jacques Doucet, has this dedication in Valéry's handwriting: "Mais ce n'est pas Racine qui signe cet exemplaire / C'est moi Paul Valéry déraciné."

187. "*The World as Will and Idea*": Arthur Schopenhauer, *Die Welt als Wille und Vorstellung* (Leipzig, 1819).

196. AT THE LAMOUREUX CONCERT IN 1893: "Allocution" given on January 4, 1931, for the fiftieth anniversary of the Lamoureux Concerts; Paris, *Commerce*, XXVI, Winter 1930; reprinted under the title "Au Concert Lamoureux en 1893," in *Pièces sur l'art*, Paris, Maurice Darantière, 1934; see *Œuvres II*, Pléiade (1960), p. 1272. Translated here by David Paul.

Lamoureux: Charles Lamoureux (1834–99), first violinist and conductor at the Paris Opera and the Opéra Comique. His fame arose from the great series of symphony concerts known as the Concerts Lamoureux, which he founded in 1881 and conducted throughout the 80's and 90's. On May 3, 1887, at the Eden Theatre, he staged the first operatic performance of *Lohengrin* in Paris. Chauvinistic opposition prevented its repetition, but Lamoureux continued his symphonic concerts of Wagner's music, then little known in France. These brought him fame and the adoration of the elite, including Mallarmé and his circle of younger poets, Valéry among them. Before the end of the century, Lamoureux managed to stage and conduct a full operatic performance of *Tristan and Isolde*, only a few days before his death in December 1899.

M. Wolff's baton: Albert Wolff, born 1884, French conductor and composer, director of the Concerts Lamoureux from 1928.

Cirque d'Été: "Summer Amphitheatre," built in 1840

on the Champs Élysées, used for circus performances, concerts, etc. (See the note following.)

197. *the Pasdeloup concerts*: Jules Étienne Pasdeloup (1819–87), French conductor, best known for his popular concerts of classical music performed at the Cirque d'Hiver, "Winter Amphitheatre" (built in 1852).

202. ON SUICIDE: Valéry's reply to a questionnaire, "Le Suicide est-il une solution?" circulated and published by *La Révolution Surréaliste*, 1st year, No. 2, January 15, 1925; reprinted as "Suicides" in *Rhumbs (Notes et autres)*, Le Divan, 1926; *Rhumbs*, Gallimard, 1933. See *Œuvres II*, Pléiade (1960), p. 608. Translated here by Roger Shattuck.

The question was posed in this way: "People live, and die. What part does the will play in all this? It appears that they commit suicide just as they dream. This is not a moral question: *Is suicide a solution?*"

206. MUSIC HALL POETS: "Les Poètes au Music-Hall," an interview conducted by M.-H. Berger, published in the newspaper *Excelsior*, February 11, 1936. Translated here by Roger Shattuck.

210. PURE INTELLECT: "L'Esprit pur," an interview conducted by André Lang and published in *Les Annales*, June 15, 1930. Translated here by Frederick Brown.

214. *Paul Souday*: (1869–1929), French journalist and critic, official literary critic of the newspaper *Le Temps*. He wrote books on Proust, Gide, and Valéry.

INDEX

INDEX

241